# Library Technology
## REPORTS
Expert Guides to Library Systems and Services

# RDA Vocabularies for a Twenty-First-Century Data Environment

*Karen Coyle*

ALA TechSource
www.alatechsource.org

Copyright © 2010 American Library Association
All Rights Reserved.

# Library Technology REPORTS

**American Library Association**
50 East Huron St.
Chicago, IL 60611-2795 USA
www.alatechsource.org
800-545-2433, ext. 4299
312-944-6780
312-280-5275 (fax)

**Advertising Representative**
Brian Searles, Ad Sales Manager
ALA Publishing Dept.
bsearles@ala.org
312-280-5282
1-800-545-2433, ext. 5282

**ALA TechSource Editor**
Dan Freeman
dfreeman@ala.org
312-280-5413

**Copy Editor**
Judith Lauber

**Administrative Assistant**
Judy Foley
jfoley@ala.org
800-545-2433, ext. 4272
312-280-5275 (fax)

**Production and Design**
ALA Production Services: Troy D. Linker
and Karen Sheets de Gracia

Library Technology Reports (ISSN 0024-2586) is published eight times a year (January, March, April, June, July, September, October, and December) by American Library Association, 50 E. Huron St., Chicago, IL 60611. It is managed by ALA TechSource, a unit of the publishing department of ALA. Periodical postage paid at Chicago, Illinois, and at additional mailing offices. POSTMASTER: Send address changes to Library Technology Reports, 50 E. Huron St., Chicago, IL 60611.

Trademarked names appear in the text of this journal. Rather than identify or insert a trademark symbol at the appearance of each name, the authors and the American Library Association state that the names are used for editorial purposes exclusively, to the ultimate benefit of the owners of the trademarks. There is absolutely no intention of infringement on the rights of the trademark owners.

ALA TechSource
www.alatechsource.org

Copyright ©2010 American Library Association
All Rights Reserved.

## About the Author

Karen Coyle is a librarian and a consultant in the area of digital libraries. She worked for over twenty years at the University of California in the California Digital Library, has served on library and information standards committees, and has written frequently on technical topics including metadata development, technology management, and system design and on policy areas like copyright and privacy.

## Abstract

Library data has been designed to be read and interpreted by librarians and users. Although there are some controlled data fields, most of what is in the library catalog entry is text. The machine as user has not gotten a great deal of attention in the library cataloging environment. Now there's yet another potential user of library data, and that user is the Web and services that function on the Web. If we are to serve our users, then we need to deliver library services to users via the Web. But delivery over the network is not enough; our services must not only be *on* the Web, but need to be *of* the Web. With Web-based data, we can use the vast information resources there to enhance our data by creating relationships between library data and information resources. This will increase not only opportunities for users to discover the library and its resources, but also the value of the data by allowing its use in a wide variety of contexts.

The idea that library metadata will be used widely on the open Web changes the meaning of cataloging: cataloging will no longer be limited to the creation of records for the library catalog; the data will serve other functions as well, and users who may never directly make use of the

## Subscriptions

For more information about subscriptions and individual issues for purchase, call the ALA Customer Service Center at 1-800-545-2433 and press 5 for assistance, or visit www.alatechsource.org.

# Table of Contents

## Chapter 1—Library Data in the Web World — 5
- Library Data — 6
- Time of Opportunity — 6
- Library Data Today — 7
- Moving Forward — 9
- Steps to Linked Data — 10
- Notes — 11

## Chapter 2—Metadata Models of the World Wide Web — 12
- Ontologies — 13
- RDF Knowledge Representation — 13
- Metadata in RDF — 15
- Some Metadata Implementations Using RDF — 17
- RDF and Library Data — 19
- Notes — 36

## Chapter 3—FRBR, the Domain Model — 20
- Entities and Relationships — 20
- Beyond *R* Is for Record — 23
- FRBR as Beta — 24
- Notes — 25

## Chapter 4—RDA in RDF — 26
- RDA Background — 27
- RDA in RDF — 27
- Maintenance of the Metadata Standard — 31
- RDA Vocabularies and the Bibliographic Record — 33
- Application Profiles — 35
- A Word about the Future — 35
- Notes — 36

## Resources — 37

**Abstract (cont.)**

library catalog. This is a true expansion of the role of library data, to the point where it can be used for any bibliographic function. However, the effort of cataloging need not increase: instead, the sharing of data can increase, and with some forethought the act of cataloging can draw on cooperative data sources. To be sure, redesign of cataloging systems will be needed.

There are four steps that must be taken in order to enter into the world of linked data: defining the data model, defining the data elements, defining the data vocabularies, and developing rules for data application. This issue of *Library Technology Reports* provides an explanation, using concrete models and real-world examples, of how to facilitate this transformation.

# Chapter 1

# Library Data in the Web World

## Abstract

*Library data has been designed to be read and interpreted by the librarians and users who are the end users of the catalog. Today's data, however, needs to be managed and interpreted by computers and integrated into myriad applications that are part of the growing web of services on the Internet. In particular, the Semantic Web technologies being developed put a new emphasis on linking data from disparate sources. To be part of the linked data network, the library world needs to transform its catalog records into true data.*

> In many respects, the most important question for the library world in examining semantic web technologies is whether librarians can successfully transform their expertise in working with metadata into expertise in working with ontologies or models of knowledge. Whereas traditional library metadata has always been focused on helping humans find and make use of information, semantic web ontologies are focused on helping machines find and make use of information. Traditional library metadata is meant to be seen and acted on by humans, and as such has always been an uncomfortable match with relational database technology. Semantic web ontologies, in contrast, are meant to make metadata meaningful and actionable for machines. An ontology is thus a sort of computer program, and the effort of making an RDF schema is the first step of telling a computer how to process a type of information.
>
> —Eric Hellman[1]

As is always the case in a time of transition, it may be possible to see where we have come from, but it is very difficult, perhaps impossible, to know where we are going. This report should thus be accepted as one moment in the path of moving target. This is how it looks to me today, and tomorrow is a different story.

When I talk about library data and the semantic web, people ask me if I really think that the Semantic Web (note the case change) and RDF are "the answer." I don't. In fact, I have no more idea of what "the answer" is or could be than most people. I do think that the move toward an open declaration of vocabularies and the freeing of data from databases and even from records is key to expanding the discovery and navigation services that we can provide to information seekers. I have no reluctance in taking from the Semantic Web movement that which seems to benefit libraries without taking in the whole. Perhaps I should have written this entire report without using the "S– W–" words, but it would have been awkward to do so purely from a view of sentence construction. When I say "Semantic Web," try to understand that I mean a set of evolving techniques for presenting data in a way that could be used on networks; those networks could be the World Wide Web or a new form of library user tool.

The work to define the data elements of the new cataloging rules, Resource Description and Access (RDA), in a Semantic Web–compatible format would not have happened without the interest of the members of the Dublin Core Metadata Initiative, who have been dipping their metadata toes into the waters of Semantic Web thinking for a number of years. It also would not have happened without the interest shared by members of the Joint Steering Committee for RDA, in particular Barbara Tillett

(Library of Congress) and Tom Delsey (RDA Editor), who attended the meeting where it all happened. Diane Hillmann (Metadata Management Associates) and Gordon Dunsire (University of Strathclyde) were given the dubious honor of managing the project, and, along with Jon Phipps (Metadata Management Associates) and myself, have completed the recommended tasks that came out of the 2007 meeting referenced above. It is worth reproducing here the report from that decisive meeting, against which our work can be measured.

The picture of data, and of library data in particular, has changed considerably in the two and half years of the project. There has been a co-evolution of RDA and the Semantic Web. The only thing we can know for sure is that the evolution will continue. Please keep that in mind as you read on.

## Library Data

Library data has been designed to be read and interpreted by librarians and users. Although there are some controlled data fields, most of what is in the library catalog entry is text. The emphasis is on the human user, even though the data today is stored in computer systems and displayed on a screen. The machine as user has not gotten a great deal of attention in the library cataloging environment.

Now there's yet another potential user of library data, and that user is the Web and services that function on the Web. We know that our users go to the Web to do their research, to interact with other people, and to create their works. If we are to serve our users, then we need to deliver library services to users via the Web. But delivery over the network is not enough; our services must not only be *on* the Web, but need to be *of* the Web. The services can not just pass through, but must live and interact on the Web. With Web-based data, we can use the vast information resources there to enhance our data by creating relationships between library data and information resources. This will not only increase opportunities for users to discover the library and its resources, but will also increase the value of the data by allowing its use in a wide variety of contexts. If you take the view that information has value when it is used, then greater use means greater value.

## Time of Opportunity

In 1837, the British Museum found itself without a printed catalog of its books. This fact became a great opportunity that was seized upon by Sir Anthony Panizzi. It was for the creation of this catalog that he developed the "Code Panizzi" consisting of ninety-one rules for the cataloging

---

**The following are notes from a data model meeting held at the British Library in London from April 30 to May 1, 2007[2]**

A meeting was held which examined the fit between *RDA: Resource Description and Access* and models used in other metadata communities.

*Participants:*

- Tom Baker
- Robina Clayphan
- Tom Delsey
- Gordon Dunsire
- Diane Hillmann
- Alistair Miles
- Mikael Nilsson
- Andy Powell
- Barbara Tillett

*Recommendations:*

The meeting participants agreed that RDA and DCMI should work together to build on the existing work of both communities.

The participants recommend that the RDA Committee of Principals and DCMI seek funding for work to develop an RDA Application Profile -- specifically that the following activities be undertaken:

- development of an RDA Element Vocabulary
- development of an RDA DC Application Profile based on FRBR and FRAD
- disclosure of RDA Value Vocabularies using RDF/RDFS/SKOS

*Outcomes:*

The benefits of this activity will be that:

- the library community gets a metadata standard that is compatible with the Web Architecture and that is fully interoperable with other Semantic Web initiatives
- the DCMI community gets a libraries application profile firmly based on the DCAM and FRBR (which will be a high profile exemplar for others to follow)
- the Semantic Web community get a significant pool of well thought-out metadata terms to re-use
- there is wider uptake of RDA

*Further suggestion:*

The meeting further suggests that DCMI and DC Application Profile developers consider the value of using conceptual models such as FRBR as the basis for describing intellectual or artistic creations.

of books.[3] Thus, modern library cataloging was born.

We also find ourselves in a time of opportunity—not because we lack a catalog but because the cataloging community has stepped back to rethink its work. The Functional Requirements for Bibliographic Records (FRBR) and Resource Description and Access (RDA) provide new models and new rules,[4] and they come at a time when the way data is stored and managed has resulted in an entirely new technology with which we can distribute our catalog entries and make them available to users. That technology is the World Wide Web, and more specifically the burgeoning use of the linked data standard to facilitate interconnections between information resources. The Web provides a platform for linking information resources regardless of their provenance.

Neither FRBR nor RDA was developed to meet the linked data standard, but the FRBR model uses entities (things) and relationships, which is conceptually similar to the basic concepts of the Semantic Web. We are in the fortunate position of having a good model for the transformation of our data to this more modern standard.

Before setting out some steps that we can take to further this transformation, it may help us to look at our current data models and systems, with an eye to identifying those areas that are functioning today as barriers to full and open use of the great store of library metadata.

*Linked Data website*
http://linkeddata.org

## Library Data Today

Library metadata has its purpose in the creation of the catalog. In fact, metadata creation is called "cataloging"—the development of a catalog. The catalog, which was originally physical but is now digital, uses database technology in a stand-alone system. Internet and Web access to the catalog is through a tunnel from the network to the database interface residing on the library system.

The catalog supports many library management functions: inventory control, collection development, acquisitions, new materials check-in, budget management, and many others. It also serves user functions such as circulation of materials, account management, and placement of hold requests. But the public thinks of the catalog primarily in its role in discovery, identification, and delivery of data. The discovery component, however, is used less and less as information and document seekers find that the Internet gives them a broader view of the information space and satisfies their needs more readily than the library catalog. Catalog uses by information seekers are an increasingly small percentage of discovery actions.[5]

Library catalog data could, however, be the connection between the library and the knowledge space on the Web. The library catalog data could be a source of quality bibliographic information for many user tasks like managing bibliographies, sharing with colleagues, and making connections between library and nonlibrary resources. For this to be the case, however, the library's bibliographic metadata needs to be "of the Web."

## Bibliographic Control

Library cataloging has historically been all about getting control over the bibliographic universe, knowing exactly what works and editions a library holds, and making sure that all items in the library catalog are uniformly described. One of the discussion points of the Task Group on the Future of Bibliographic Control was the question the use of the term *bibliographic control*. The group defined the term as "the organization of library materials to facilitate discovery, management, identification, and access."[6] The group also said, however:

> The phrase "bibliographic control" is often interpreted to have the same meaning as the word "cataloging." The library catalog, however, is just one access route to materials that a library manages for its users. The benefits of bibliographic control can be expanded to a wide range of information resources both through cooperation and through design. The Working Group urges adoption of a broad definition of bibliographic control that embraces all library materials, a diverse community of users, and a multiplicity of venues where information is sought.[7]

In this statement, the Working Group opened up the possibility that in the future bibliographic control may be more than what we think of today as cataloging and may take place beyond the confines of the library catalog. They confirm this with another statement:

> The future of bibliographic control will be collaborative, decentralized, international in scope, and Web-based. Its realization will occur in cooperation with the private sector, and with the active collaboration of library users. Data will be gathered from multiple sources; change will happen quickly; and bibliographic control will be dynamic, not static. The underlying technology that makes this future possible and necessary—the World Wide Web—is now almost two decades old. Libraries must continue the transition to this future without delay in order to retain their significance as information providers.[8]

There is much here to frighten anyone who hopes that the library catalog will need just some minor tweaking to keep up with modern times. It's pretty clear, though, that the group was defining bibliographic control to mean something quite different from the creation of library catalogs as we know them today. Their expanded definition and the emphasis on the World Wide Web as the appropriate platform for reaching today's users greatly broaden the role that library metadata will have to fulfill.

### Bibliographic Data on the Web

There is an increasing use of bibliographic data on the Web in general, through services like Google Scholar and Google Book Search, Wikipedia and Wikimedia, LibraryThing, Open Library, and others. Some of these directly import library metadata, others create their own. The content of these sites is not limited to bibliographic data; they use bibliographic data within an information context. In some cases, the object of the bibliographic metadata is the focus of the document or page; in other cases, it serves as a pointer to other resources. In either case, though, it is clear that resources cataloged by libraries are part of the online information landscape. That landscape, however, does not make use of the MARC record, and there is no unifying standard for bibliographic data. There also is no concrete way to link data on the Web with the many instances of that data in library catalogs. Where specific item or record identifiers, such as ISBN or OCLC number, are available, it is often possible to link through WorldCat to library holdings, but that is a viable option only for OCLC member libraries and also doesn't provide links from other data elements to the bibliographic data. It is a partial implementation of integration of library bibliographic data to the Web, but only partial.

The idea that library metadata will be used widely on the open Web changes the meaning of cataloging: cataloging will no longer be limited to the creation of records for the library catalog, but will serve other functions as well, and users who may never directly make use of the library catalog. This is a true expansion of the role of library data, to the point where it can be used for any bibliographic function. However, the effort of cataloging need not increase: instead, the sharing of data can increase, and with some forethought the act of cataloging can draw on cooperative data sources. To be sure, redesign of cataloging systems will be needed.

### Data in Records

Library metadata is, and has always been, a complex concept with many different points of information. Both technically and in terms of information content, the library record must be used as a whole. The record provides the context for each data element, and holds together all of the fields that describe a particular manifestation. A field taken out of this context would not be meaningful. A field like the following is not useful because it is only within the record that we know to what book it refers:

260 $a New York : $b Viking Penguin, $c 1994

The exact same information can be designed to have meaning both within a record and independently. This is done by providing explicit relationships and identifiers for the subject of the description:

New York → is place of publication of → Raintree County

Viking Penguin → is publisher of → Raintree County

1994 → is date of publication of → Raintree County

This form of data allows processing on individual data elements within their meaningful context. It creates more possibilities for machines to act on the data. For example, you may wish to know the earliest date of publication of a book, at least the earliest that the library has. With this type of data organization, it is possible to ask for all of the dates of publication for the book in question, and to receive the following as an answer:

1948

1994

Note that where the above examples have meaningful words ("Raintree County," "is publisher of"), the actual data would have identifiers for those terms and concepts. This is because the words themselves could be ambiguous ("Raintree County" is both a book and a film, and each would need its own identifier), and in any case they are not globally unique. Someone else could develop a term "is publisher of" that has a meaning slightly different from the one that I am using. The unique identification of *things* and *relationships* assures that data can mix with other data without losing its specific meaning.

All of this facilitates machine processing, of course, but it also potentially provides some new capabilities for user interfaces as well. It should be much easier to create a function that will find other editions of the same book without requiring that the user perform a search. For example, if the user has entered the catalog from a link on a professor's reading list and all copies of the book are checked out, it should be possible to expand the search to the most recent other edition of the book. In a library catalog today, the user would need to perform a search and either read through a list of retrieved items or limit by date. With the catalog record reorganized in a linked data format, this becomes an automated offering, not a user task. The main reason to organize our data as separate and unambiguous data elements, however, is to allow that data to be used outside of the context of the library catalog and to be combined with other data.

Fortunately, the data in library records is coded in some detail, so a transformation from the record-based model to a data-based model is feasible. The whole of the information about a single item may still be wrapped together as a record, but the data within that record will be usable in many different contexts.

## Database as Container

The closed system model used by libraries is related to the dependence on a record-based model. This has been the dominant model for all forms of data, not just in libraries. In a database management system, data is stored in a highly controlled environment with specific functions allowed to different categories of users: those who can modify the database management structure (the system administrators), those who can modify records (the catalogers), and those who can enter only through the user interface (the users). Regardless of how rich the data, users of this system can perform only actions that are offered to them through the interface.

In addition, the data in the database cannot easily interact with data outside of the database. Libraries have added some links to Web services and are able to import book covers and reviews from other sources, but dynamic interaction is difficult to achieve. It can even be impossible to link into the library catalog from outside, thus limiting users' ability to make reference to items held in the library. This means that library data cannot participate in the highly linked and linkable information environment on the Web, and this limits the visibility of libraries to Web users.

## The Search as Discovery

Users go to the library catalog to search for items in the library collection. To conduct a search, they must have something in mind: an author, a title, or a topic. Searching is a familiar first step in information seeking, but it is not the only way, and perhaps not even the predominant way, that users find the information they need. In real life—that is, "offline"—friends, colleagues, and mass media are common leads to information sources. Online, social sites have become powerful meeting grounds where users ask questions, find recommendations, and pursue a wide variety of interests. While it may be difficult to think of these actions as "information retrieval," they do provide users with a great deal of information. Just because a person stumbles upon an interesting site or reads a book that is recommended by a friend does not mean that no information has been exchanged. These informal sources of information are not at all new: many experts cite other members of their profession as their main source of information and commonly begin an investigation in a new area by contacting a colleague who is already expert in that area.

Offline, we rely on a web of human connections to help us find information. Online, that web consists of links between resources and rich social interaction that help us select and evaluate resources. The search itself is only a beginning. The library catalog, however, offers little beyond search and retrieve. Navigation is generally limited to clicking on headings, which then performs another search. The catalog, therefore, serves only limited information-seeking behavior. It is no wonder that few users report that they begin their information searches in the library catalog and that the use of library catalogs is minor compared to the use of the Internet.

It is unlikely that searching will be eliminated from our information discovery toolkit, but we can expect that navigation capabilities will become increasingly available as more and more information moves to the Web. Today we follow links found within documents, but the Semantic Web promises even richer navigation possibilities, as well as the ability to actually pose questions to the Web, treating it much like a database of information.

## Moving Forward

Libraries already have the key elements for a modern metadata definition: there is a general model of the library domain provided by the FRBR entities, relationships, and attributes; there is a statement of goals in the FRBR user tasks; and a detailed set of data elements, vocabularies, and guidance rules exists in library cataloging standards, most recently in RDA. The FRBR model and the cataloging rules are coherent with each other to the extent that RDA assigns data elements to the FRBR entities.

Both FRBR and RDA are realized as documents, which means that they are presented as human-readable concepts, not as computer code. In their document forms, neither can be acted on by computers, and neither can be moved seamlessly into the Web. It may not even be possible to turn them into code without some significant changes. But the use of entities and relationships gives this whole that is FRBR + RDA some basic conceptual compatibility with the technology that is developing for the realization of the Semantic Web.

One of the first steps that needs to be taken is to tease out the many components that are encompassed by the RDA text. RDA is not a single unit but in fact a combination of

- the elements of bibliographic description
- the relationships between those elements and between areas of description
- the rules for deciding what data will be used to describe bibliographic items

All of this is wrapped up together in our cataloging rules, which makes it very hard to turn them into a machine-usable set of elements. The RDA development committee did create a list of data elements and relationships, but it pulled these out of the text; it didn't build the text on them. Machines, however, will act on the data elements, not on the explanatory text, so it will be necessary to look at the data elements carefully to discover any areas where the creation of machine processing may not fit in with what is written in the text. This is because there are concepts you can create in text that you cannot automate directly. When creating text, it is hard to know when you are relying on human intelligence to make leaps that a computer cannot. The guidance rules and the data structures need to be developed together if the machine processing is going to be successful. There is going to have to be some back and forth between data structures and rules for decision making to be sure that we've covered both the human and the machine needs.

These functions need to be teased apart in order to create Semantic Web–compatible data. This is because the Semantic Web requires certain information about data elements. Some of this information may be inherent in the RDA text, such as a rule that a cataloged item will have only one preferred title, or that dates may be entered in a structured format. All of this information needs to be made explicit in the definition of the elements for use in machine processing.

## Steps to Linked Data

There are four basic steps that one needs to take to enter into the world of linked data, data that can play well on the Semantic Web. The first is to design the basic data model. We have that already in the form of the definitions of functional requirements in FRBR, FRAD, and others. These models will undoubtedly undergo some evolution as library data and the data environment change. The second is to define the data elements (or, in Semantic Web parlance, *properties)* of our metadata. Part of this process is making those definitions available on the Web in a machine-actionable format. The third major step is to define all of our controlled lists in a linked data compatible format and to also make those available on the Web for anyone to use and to provide definitions and display capabilities.

### 1. Define the Model

We talked above about the FRBR model and the user tasks that have guided its development. A great value of the family of functional requirements is that they begin to define the entities that our metadata addresses: bibliographic resources, agents, topics. At this level, we can see some similarities already with linked data standards being developed elsewhere. For example, an early Semantic Web project is "Friend of a Friend" (FOAF), a metadata format for persons that can be used in social network situations.[9] It is not identical to the way that libraries define persons, but it points to an area where data could be exchanged among different communities.

### 2. Define Data Elements

This step is similar to the initial creation of a database structure, where you define all of your data elements. Each data element will need to be defined according to certain requirements posed by the Semantic Web concepts. The Semantic Web view of data differs from that of a database, so developers will need some level of learning and adjustment.

### 3. Define Vocabularies

One of the great advantages that we have in transforming our catalog data to the Semantic Web is that we have already made much use of controlled vocabularies. These help greatly in communicating with other communities because we can clearly delineate the possible meanings of certain elements through the finite vocabulary list that the element can carry.

Vocabularies can be simple lists of terms, but it is also possible to define each term in a vocabulary with a unique identifier. Identifiers are less ambiguous than language and also often create links back to the identifying agency and documentation about the term. For example, the term *green* can mean different things: in the context of politics, it may indicate an approach toward environmental issues or even the name of a political party. In a shoe catalog, it may be the color of the product. The use of an identifier provided by the entity that has developed the vocabulary means that each of these meanings will have a different identifier.

### 4. Develop Application Rules

There is another level of definition that will usually be undertaken, although it is not strictly required by the Semantic Web, and that is the creation of application rules or an application profile. Application rules generally add constraints to your metadata, such as whether your element will be mandatory or optional, and rules for repeatability. For example, although you may define the element for title in your list of elements, yet in your actual application you may wish to limit the use of the title to one per description. Or you may wish to say that in your application the title is mandatory. The definition of these rules in a machine-readable form will allow others to understand the output of your applications.

The remainder of this report will illustrate these steps in greater detail.

## Notes

1. Eric Hellman. "Can Librarians Be Put Directly onto the Semantic Web?" Go to Hellman blog, Aug. 4, 2009, http://go-to-hellman.blogspot.com/2009/08/can-librarians-be-put-directly-onto.html (accessed Dec. 14, 2009).
2. British Library, "Data Model Meeting," www.bl.uk/bibliographic/meeting.html (accessed December 14th, 2009.
3. Anthony Panizzi, "Rules for the Compilation of the Catalogue," *Catalogue of Printed Books in the British Museum*, vol. 1 (London: 1841), v–ix.
4. IFLA Study Group on the Functional Requirements for Bibliographic Records, *Functional Requirements for Bibliographic Records: Final Report*, Sept. 1997, as amended and corrected through Feb. 2009, http://archive.ifla.org/VII/s13/frbr/frbr_2008.pdf (accessed Dec. 14, 2009); Joint Steering Committee for Development of RDA, "RDA: Resource Description and Access," www.rda-jsc.org/rda.html (accessed Dec. 14, 2009).
5. Cathy De Rosa, *Perceptions of Libraries and Information Resources: A Report to the OCLC Membership* (Dubin, OH: OCLC Online Computer Library Center, 2005), 1–17.
6. *On the Record: Report of the Library of Congress Working Group on the Future of Bibliographic Control* (Washington, DC: Library of Congress, 2008), 6; available online at www.loc.gov/bibliographic-future/news/lcwg-ontherecord-jan08-final.pdf (accessed Nov. 6, 2009).
7. *On the Record*, 10.
8. *On the Record*, 4.
9. Dan Brickley and Libby Miller, "FOAF Vocabulary Specification 0.97," The FOAF Project website, http://xmlns.com/foaf/spec (accessed Jan. 5, 2010).

Chapter 2

# Metadata Models of the World Wide Web

## Abstract

*The Semantic Web, in standards being developed by the World Wide Web Consortium, is a new way of defining metadata for use and reuse in a networked environment. In this chapter of "RDA Vocabularies for a Twenty-First-Century Data Environment," we'll discuss the definition of metadata and how it involves the creation of domain models (the things and relationships that the metadata will describe) and ontologies (the vocabularies that the metadata will use). The use of standard identifiers, called Uniform Resource Identifiers, creates unambiguous identities for data and statements about data.*

The World Wide Web was developed as a web of documents. On this Web, digital documents would link to each other directly, allowing the user to follow the pointers provided by the author from a place in one document to another digital document. In hindsight, it seems obvious that while this ability to navigate the hyperlinks provided is extraordinarily powerful (and achieved something that is not possible in the analog world), the model lacked a key component for discovery, and that is meaningful metadata for the documents themselves. This problem has been partially overcome by the development of search engines that can index the actual text of the documents. Keyword indexing on uncontrolled text, however, lacks precision for searching.

The *Semantic Web* is a result of the realization that there is information in the documents on the Web that could be extremely valuable if it could be made actionable—that is, if there were a way to interact with the information inside documents, not just the documents themselves.[1] The emphasis of the Semantic Web is on topical information within the Web resources: information about persons, places, things, events, and covering the full range of scientific and humanistic thought. To turn the web of documents into a web of data, the Web needs metadata to represent that information. This metadata will not look like standard bibliographic metadata. Bibliographic metadata represents a document or resource. The purpose of the Semantic Web is not to create metadata that represents documents or resources; it is to create metadata for the informational content of those resources.

While Web documents resemble the granularity of articles more than that of books, there is significant overlap in the topics covered by the Web and by libraries. Yet these remain two separate and distinct information spheres. In part this is because libraries hold primarily physical resources. Yet where libraries and the Web could collaborate through an intermingling of digital resources, they are unable to because they use different technologies. The Web relies entirely on search engines and keyword searches, while libraries create metadata in a library-specific record format (MARC) that is stored in closed databases. The development of metadata solutions that are compatible with Web-based technology and can be used both by libraries and on the open Web creates the possibility of making a connection between the two worlds.

In relation to libraries, the Web community is quite late in realizing the importance of metadata. There may have been an advantage to starting to think about metadata for the first time in a fully automated environment. The Semantic Web community began with a kind of metadata *tabula rasa* and a natural tendency to think about machine processing of data at a deep level. Its work began with a study of the basic nature of metadata, or at least the very nature of machine-actionable, networked, interoperable metadata.

Similar to the development of the underlying standards that make the Internet possible, such as TCP/IP, the Semantic Web developers sought to develop the basic structure on which all other metadata would be developed. This basic structure is called the Resource Description Framework, or RDF. RDF itself relies on the Uniform Resource Identifier, the standard identifier format for the Web, and eXtensible Markup Language (XML), a set of rules for encoding documents and data electronically. These form the bottom layer of the "layer cake" of Semantic Web standards (see figure 1).

*Resource Description Framework (RDF): W3C Semantic Web Activity*
www.w3.org/RDF

## Ontologies

To participate in the Semantic Web, a community needs to define an ontology. An ontology, in the sense used by the developers of the Semantic Web, defines the metadata for a particular slice of the knowledge universe. That slice is called a *domain*. Ontologies include a conceptualization of the elements of the domain and the relationships between those elements. The elements, called *entities* in Semantic Web parlance, can be things or concepts. The expression of the ontology creates a controlled vocabulary for describing entities in the domain. The goal is a rigorous knowledge base that can be subjected to computation. Ontologies differ from traditional thesauri and taxonomies primarily in being designed specifically for machine processing, as well as their use of a large variety of relationships between the entities in the defined domain.

The use of relationships in Semantic Web technology adds another dimension to the way the knowledge domain is defined. Where taxonomies are generally two-dimensional and organized in a hierarchy, ontologies can make use of relationships beyond the parent-child relationships that hierarchy implies. Ontologies can express temporal relationships (A happens before B), positional relationships (A is near B), causal relationships (A creates B), and any other relationship you can imagine.

As an example, Ian Davis and Eric Vitiello have created a vocabulary for describing relationships between people that they call simply "RELATIONSHIP." The vocabulary contains thirty-five possible relationships, from family relationships ("grandparent of") to less stable relationships ("has met," "would like to know").

*RELATIONSHIP: A Vocabulary for Describing Relationships between People*
http://vocab.org/relationship/.html

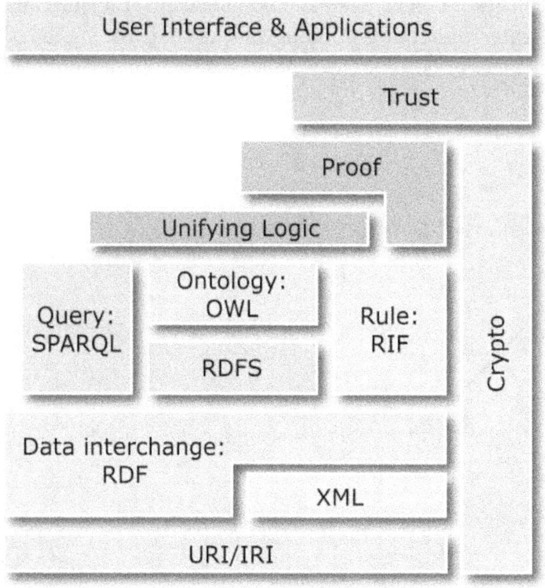

The Resource Description Framework (RDF) is the Semantic Web standard for defining an ontology in machine-readable form.

## RDF Knowledge Representation

In some ways, RDF reflects classic thinking about the nature of knowledge and how we represent it. It models knowledge as classes of things and relationships between things. Members of a class all have the characteristics that define the class.

### The Role of Identifiers

Although RDF is described in terms that can also be expressed in human language (*subject, object*), what distinguishes it from natural language is that it is intended to be processed by machines. For that reason, RDF does not make use of natural language for the concepts and things it describes. Instead, each element of the RDF statement must be expressed with a unique identifier. This unique identifier has two primary advantages: (1) it overcomes the inherent ambiguity of human language (Pluto the celestial body vs. Pluto the Disney character)

**Figure 1**
The Semantic Web "layer cake" model. Source: www.w3.org/2007/03/layerCake.png (accessed Dec. 15, 2009). Copyright © 2007 World Wide Web Consortium (Massachusetts Institute of Technology, European Research Consortium for Informatics and Mathematics, Keio University). All Rights Reserved. http://www.w3.org/Consortium/Legal/2002/copyright-documents-20021231.

| URI | What It Identifies |
|---|---|
| http://purl.org/dc/terms/title | the Dublin Core metadata term "title" |
| http://id.loc.gov/authorities/sh85103579 | the LC subject authority entry for "Pluto (Dwarf planet)" |
| http://id.loc.gov/authorities/sh96010495 | the LC subject authority entry for "Pluto (Fictitious character)" |
| http://xmlns.com/foaf/spec/#term_name | the Friend of a Friend vocabulary term for a name |

**Table 1**
Examples of identifiers used on the Web and the Semantic Web.

| Subject | Predicate | Object |
|---|---|---|
| Vladimir Nabokov | is author of | *Lolita* |

**Table 2**
"Vladimir Nabokov is the author of *Lolita*"

| Subject | Predicate | Object |
|---|---|---|
| http://en.wikipedia.org/wiki/Vladimir_Nabokov | http://rdvocab.info/roles/authorWork | http://lccn.loc.gov/56024827 |

**Table 3**
Nabokov statement with URIs.

and (2) it allows for internationalization of the metadata, because the same identifier can be used even though the language of the display form is different (*computer* versus *ordinateur*).

On the Web, the standard identifier is called a Uniform Resource Identifier (URI). A URI follows a prescribed syntax: it begins with a URI scheme name, followed by a colon, followed by a string in a format that is particular to that scheme. It so happens that the URL, with its "http:" at the beginning, is a valid URI. URLs are commonly used as identifiers in Web-compatible applications (see table 1).

### Statements

The basic building block of RDF is the *statement*. RDF statements are semantic units in a simple form: subject + predicate + object. Like simple molecules, the statements are interconnecting building blocks that can create complex networks. A statement says something simple, like

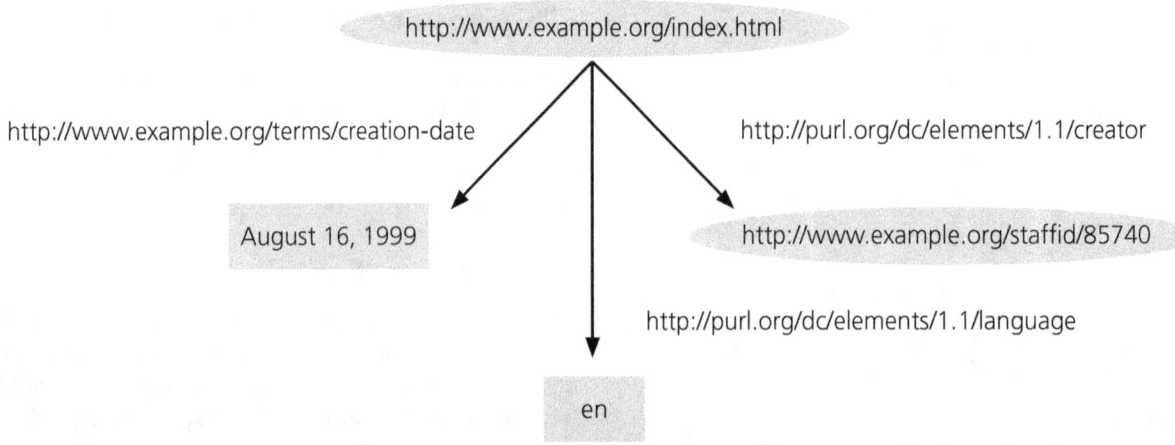

**Figure 2**
A simple RDF diagram. Source: "RDF Primer: W3C Recommendation 10 February 2004," figure 3, www.w3.org/TR/rdf-primer (accessed Dec. 15, 2009). Copyright © 2004 World Wide Web Consortium (Massachusetts Institute of Technology, European Research Consortium for Informatics and Mathematics, Keio University). All Rights Reserved. http://www.w3.org/Consortium/Legal/2002/copyright-documents-20021231.

**Figure 3**
*Lolita* information represented in RDF graph.

"Vladimir Nabokov is the author of *Lolita*" (see table 2).

Note that in actual machine-readable RDF, each element of the statement would be represented by a URI (see table 3).

Because each statement is made up of three parts, they are often referred to as *triples*. Statements are commonly represented with diagrams (see figure 2).

Because using accurate URIs would make the examples in this document difficult to read, most examples that follow will use abbreviated values in the place of actual URIs.

With current library data in MARC21 records, the same data is present but expressed differently, in part because of the record structure that binds separate statements to each other. In a MARC21 record, the two statements below are semantically the same as the RDF graph shown in figure 3.

    100 $a Nabokov, Vladimir

    245 $a Lolita

What differs, and significantly so, is that the RDF statement contains the authorship relationship explicitly, while the two separate fields in the MARC21 record are held together only because they are contained within the same record. Outside of the record structure, they lose their connection to each other. The explicit inclusion of the relationship between the two things in our statement, the name of the person and the title of the book, creates a meaningful information unit that is not dependent on a record format.

## Metadata in RDF

The Resource Description Framework is neither a data format nor an application. RDF provides a basic level of structure for metadata on which actual metadata can be built. It is so simple that it defines only three types of data that can be used in a statement: literal values (free text), structured values (text, but with structure like date and time), and identifiers in URI format. While the first two are essentially kinds of strings, the last can represent anything that has a Web-compatible identifier.

The Dublin Core Metadata Initiative built its abstract model (DCAM) on top of RDF and added a few more details that could be of use in library metadata. In particular, DCAM adds values that are controlled vocabularies.

### Value Types

#### Literal

When an element is defined as taking a literal value, it means that the value will be free text, such as titles of documents, descriptive notes, or reviews. Knowing that this element will be free text tells developers that there is limited "computing" that can be applied to the data. This is a field for human readers, not for specific machine processing. The developer then needs to understand the meaning and intent of the field in order to determine how and when to present it to users, whether it might be useful as a searchable field, and so on.

#### Structured Value

A structured string is one with a defined set of elements, like "yyyy-mm-dd" for a date. There may be value rules, such as limiting the characters allowed to numbers and hyphens. The structure often allows for certain operations to be performed, like presenting the data in an ordered list either alphabetically or numerically. Structure is also valuable for the creation of displays. For example, "2009-02-14" could be displayed as "February 14, 2009" or "14 febbraio, 2009" or "14/02/2009."

Application programs usually exert control over input of the data in structured strings, making sure that the data matches the defined structure perfectly so that subsequent processing will produce accurate results.

What makes up the structure can be nearly anything, including other data elements. The bibliographic element "publication statement" is a structured element consisting of the elements "place," "publisher," and "publication date," each of which could be a defined element represented by a URI.

#### URI

Oftentimes the actual value of an RDF property will be an identifier, as in the example in table 3 where we identified our book author with the URI "http://en.wikipedia.org/wiki/Vladimir_Nabokov." Where possible, this is the preferred method for representing data on the Semantic Web.

Although anyone can create URIs, their value for sharing and linking data arises from the authority of the agency assigning the identifier. The domain portion of a URL ("id.loc.gov") generally belongs to the assigning agency, which is also often the agency that has created the data being identified. Many commonly needed data types have not yet been assigned an identifier, such as standard lists for languages, and this is something of a stumbling block in the development of the Semantic Web.

### Controlled List

In the controlled list data type, the value itself is taken from a previously determined finite list. The simplest of these are lists like those for languages or language codes, musical instruments, or audience types.

Some lists have structural relationships between their entries. For example, a thesaurus is a controlled vocabulary with structural relationships between entries (broader terms, narrower terms), and it often contains alternate forms of display for the entries and definitions. The name authority files used in libraries are controlled lists in which a given name has a great deal of information associated with it in the name authority record.

Controlled lists are used in metadata creation applications to assure that the value entered is indeed one of the values on the list. Applications making use of metadata that has controlled values take advantage of additional information that is provided related to the value. To do so, however, the controlled value must be unambiguously identified, preferably with a URI, and the information must be available in a machine-readable form on the Web. The Library of Congress is the maintenance agency for many controlled lists used by library cataloging, including the Subject Authorities, which are now available defined in accordance with Semantic Web

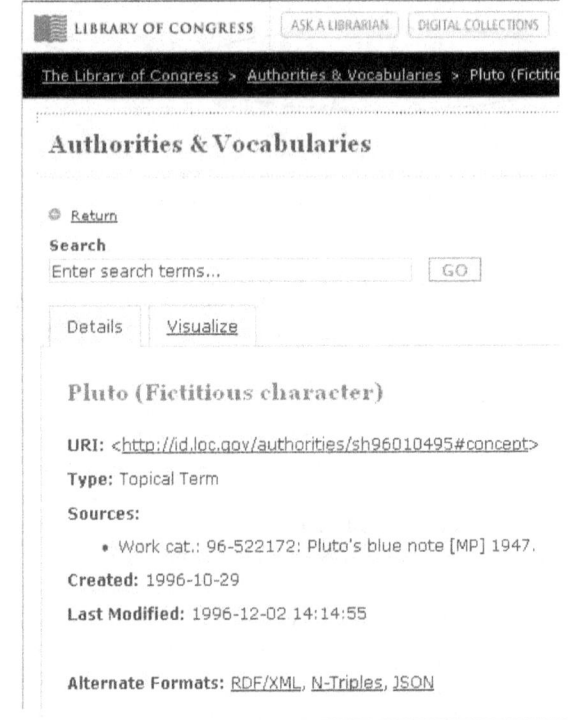

**Figure 4**
An LC subject authority entry on the Web in human-friendly format. Source: http://id.loc.gov/authorities/sh96010495.

technology. Each entry in the list has a unique identifier, and the authority record data is available for human readers and for machine processing. Figure 4 shows an LC subject authority entry in human-friendly format, and

```
<?xml version="1.0" encoding="UTF-8"?>
<rdf:RDF
    xmlns:dcterms="http://purl.org/dc/terms/"
    xmlns:owl="http://www.w3.org/2002/07/owl#"
    xmlns:rdf="http://www.w3.org/1999/02/22-rdf-syntax-ns#"
    xmlns:skos="http://www.w3.org/2004/02/skos/core#"
>
    <rdf:Description rdf:about="http://id.loc.gov/authorities/sh96010495#concept">
        <skos:prefLabel xml:lang="en">Pluto (Fictitious character)</skos:prefLabel>
        <owl:sameAs rdf:resource="info:lc/authorities/sh96010495"/>
        <dcterms:modified rdf:datatype="http://www.w3.org/2001/XMLSchema#dateTime">1996-12-02T14:14:55-04:00</dcterms:modified>
        <rdf:type rdf:resource="http://www.w3.org/2004/02/skos/core#Concept"/>
        <dcterms:created rdf:datatype="http://www.w3.org/2001/XMLSchema#dateTime">1996-10-29T00:00:00-04:00</dcterms:created>
        <dcterms:source xml:lang="en">Work cat.: 96-522172: Pluto's blue note [MP] 1947.</dcterms:source>
        <skos:inScheme rdf:resource="http://id.loc.gov/authorities#conceptScheme"/>
        <skos:inScheme rdf:resource="http://id.loc.gov/authorities#topicalTerms"/>
    </rdf:Description>
</rdf:RDF>
```

**Figure 5**
The same data as that shown in figure 4 in RDF/XML for use in computer applications.

figure 5 shows the same data in RDF/XML for use in computer applications.

## Some Metadata Implementations Using RDF

RDF provides a foundation but is not itself a metadata implementation. There are numerous metadata standards and applications that are being developed using the RDF concepts and rules. Some of the ones of greatest interest to library data developers are listed here.

### SKOS

The World Wide Web consortium (W3C), the standards body that develops Semantic Web standards and is also responsible for RDF, is creating some key data formats that use RDF. Of these, one of great importance to libraries is Simple Knowledge Organization System (SKOS). SKOS is a standard way to present organized data such as thesauri, classification schemes, and subject heading schemes. With SKOS you can represent hierarchical relationships and provide indexing terms, entry vocabulary, and definitions. Because the basis of SKOS is RDF, SKOS makes use of the RDF concepts of classes, properties, and values.

SKOS is being used for the implementation of Library of Congress Subject Headings on the Web. It is also being used for the encoding of the vocabularies that are part of the new library cataloging standard, Resource Description and Access (RDA). Both of these will be discussed in greater detail later on.

### OWL

Another W3C standard is the Web Ontology Language, OWL. OWL contains additional features for the expression of vocabularies and relationships between terms in a way that facilitates the development of machine applications that use the vocabularies. The implementations of OWL to date tends to focus on scientific vocabularies, where the precision of OWL is needed.

### Linked Data

By far the most commonly used implementation of RDF is that of linked data. Linked data is a fairly simple expression of data using the basic concepts of RDF: that data is expressed in the RDF triple format (subject–predicate–object) and that the parts of the triple should be represented by standard identifiers where available. The starting point for linked data as a concept is in a 2006 essay by Tim Berners-Lee on the W3C website.[2] In that short essay, Berners-Lee laid out the essential rules for linked data, which include the use of URLs to identify elements. One great advantage of using URLs as identifiers is that the identifier can also serve as a link to further information about the thing being identified. While using the same string as both an identifier and a location can also create some confusion, this method has been used already for hundreds of data sets.

Whereas the Semantic Web, at least as initially described by Berners-Lee, was intended to create a web

*OWL overview*
www.w3.org/TR/owl2-overview

*List of OWL ontologies*
http://protegewiki.stanford.edu/index.php/Protege_Ontology_Library

*Linked Data website*
http://linkeddata.org

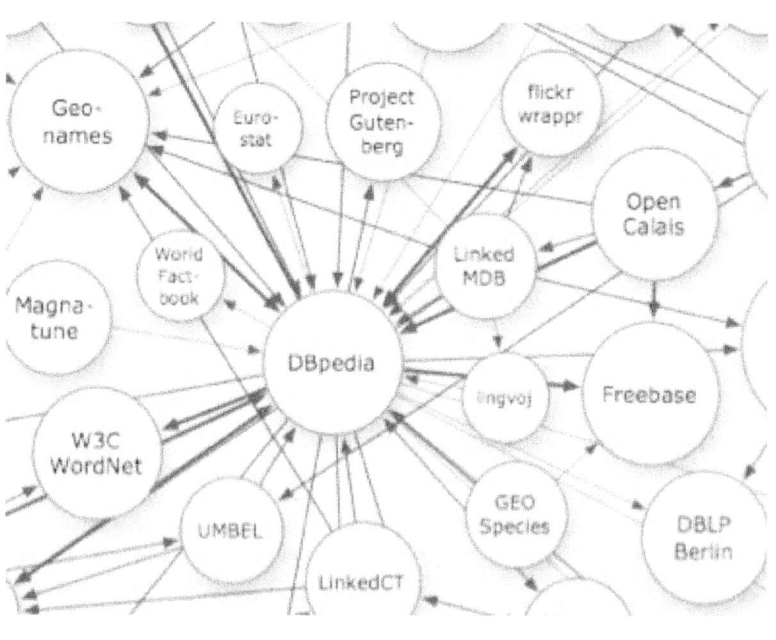

**Figure 6**
Partial view of the "linked data cloud" from http://linkeddata.org.

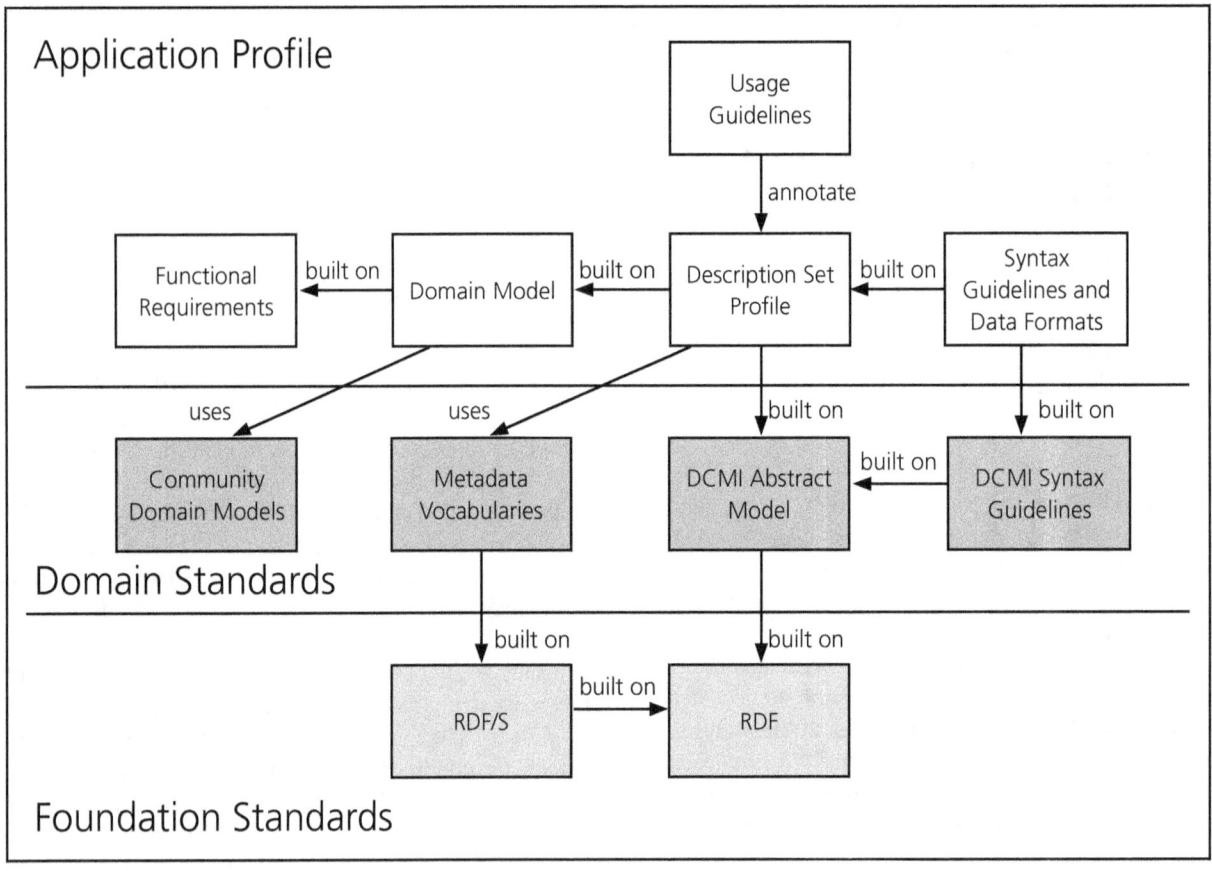

**Figure 7**
The Singapore Framework. Source: http://dublincore.org/documents/singapore-framework. Copyright © 2007 Dublin Core Metadata Initiative. All Rights Reserved. http://www.dublincore.org/about/copyright/.

from the information currently buried in the many millions (or billions?) of documents on the Web, linked data is taking on a somewhat simpler task by allowing those with data and metadata that is already in a structured format to place that data on the Web. Once on the Web in a standard format, data from different sources can be linked together to create new information views. The data available as linked data varies greatly, from data sets representing popular music and movies to scientific data like that of Bio2RDF, covering human and mouse genome information (see figure 6).

### The Dublin Core Metadata Initiative

The Dublin Core Metadata Initiative (DCMI) has embraced RDF principles in its work and has transformed the initial fifteen metadata elements that make up the original core set into an extensible and flexible RDF-compliant set of metadata.[3] Its new work goes far beyond the creation of a core of metadata elements, although the work does include the definition of the Dublin Core metadata terms using Semantic Web standards. Of particular interest is the "big picture" model with Foundation Standards, Domain Standards, and Application Profiles, shown in figure 7. The diagram is known as the Singapore Framework because it was first presented at the Dublin Core conference in Singapore in 2007.[4]

The Singapore Framework diagram helps make sense of the complex of elements that make up a functional metadata description. It also introduces the concept of an application profile as the cohesive element for metadata applications.

Some elements of the diagram are specific to the thinking of the Dublin Core community, in particular the DCMI Abstract Model and the DCMI Syntax Guidelines. The basic structure and components, however, are very helpful for understanding the creation of a metadata set in an environment where the metadata must be defined for machine processing. The foundation of the model is RDF, which provides the basic concepts of metadata components in terms of things and relationships. The next layer up defines domain standards, such as a general community domain model and the vocabularies that will be used in the application. In the library community, the Functional Requirements for Bibliographic Records (FRBR) and its companion models of Functional Requirements for Authority Data (FRAD) and Functional Requirements for Subject Authority Records (FRASAR) are the models of our domain. They specify the components and delineate the boundaries of library metadata. Above this level is that of the application profile. It is here that the somewhat abstract definition of terms and structures becomes an operational metadata activity, with a selection of terms and the presence of guidelines for the creation of metadata for that community.

## CIDOC CRM

The international museum community is also working on new models for its data under the International Council of Museums. The CIDOC Conceptual Reference Model (CRM) defines an extensible semantic framework for the scientific documentation of cultural heritage collections. The CIDOC CRM has been developed in cooperation with the DCMI and FRBR communities, among others. The CIDOC ontology for cultural heritage information has

*International Council of Museums*
http://icom.museum

*CIDOC Conceptual Reference Model, v. 5.0.1 (Nov. 2009)*
http://cidoc.ics.forth.gr/docs/cidoc_crm_version_5.0.1_Nov09.pdf

been established as ISO 21127. The CIDOC CRM ontology is available as a file in RDF.

CIDOC CRM's domain model covers description, object management, and preservation. CIDOC has also created an extension of FRBR called FRBRoo, for "object-oriented." FRBRoo has many additional entities that are required by the museum community, including entities for individual and complex works and for events. These entities reflect needs of the museum community that were not part of the library community's analysis.

The museum community is of particular interest to library metadata development because there is an overlap between the metadata needs of museums (which own objects and documents) and libraries (which own mainly documents but also some objects). The CIDOC CRM has the potential to provide an excellent testbed for the concept of linking between the library and the museum

*ISO 21127*
www.iso.org/iso/catalogue_detail.htm?csnumber=34424

*CIDOC CRM v3.3.2 Encoded in RDFS*
www.cidoc-crm.org/docs/xml_to_rdfs/CIDOC_v3.3.2.rdfs

communities using a FRBR- and RDF-based metadata model.

## RDF and Library Data

In the past, library cataloging has focused almost exclusively on the creation of usage guidelines in the form of cataloging rules. Usage guidelines are the instructions on how to make decisions about the content of the metadata. This is an area where libraries excel, and the rules cover cases that most other communities handling bibliographic data have never considered.

Until recently, a well-developed domain model did not exist, but this has been described by FRBR and its companion functional models. The addition of FRBR to the library metadata toolkit provides both an opportunity and a challenge: the opportunity to rethink the structure and content of library metadata, and the challenge to actually restructure that metadata based on that rethinking.

RDA, as an implementation of the FRBR model, provides a chance to move into a more modern style of metadata development and usage. As with previous library cataloging rules, RDA is primarily in the form of usage guidelines: a document for the catalogers who will make decisions about the content of library metadata. From the document, however, one can extract the information necessary for the creation of the metadata vocabularies.

*FRBRoo Model, v. 1.0 (draft), May 2009*
www.cidoc-crm.org/docs/frbr_oo/frbr_docs/FRBRoo_V1.0_draft__2009_may_.pdf

These vocabularies can initially be defined apart from any particular data or record format. It is the combination of the vocabularies, the model, and an eventual application profile that will form the basis for the future of bibliographic data.

The remainder of this report will focus on the possible transformation of library data through Semantic Web and linked data principles.

Continued on page 36

Chapter 3

# FRBR, the Domain Model

## Abstract

*Library metadata is already well-positioned to become part of the linked data community. The creation of the Functional Requirements for Bibliographic Records (FRBR), an entity-relation model for library data, is an essential first step for the transformation of the text-based catalog record into a true data model. FRBR may undergo some changes as libraries gain experience with it, but it allows experimentation with new data structures, and hopefully for a transition of library data to a linkable format. This chapter of "RDA Vocabularies for a Twenty-First Century Data Environment" explores FRBR and its significance.*

The Singapore Framework for Dublin Core Application Profiles includes a community model as a foundational element for the creation of a metadata set. This model informs the development of the community's metadata and also provides a schematic explanation of the community's domain to others.

For many years, library cataloging created highly detailed metadata without articulating such a conceptual model, although the cataloging rules themselves represented a mental model that was shared by trained catalogers. There was no pressing need for an explicit model while there was little desire to share library data beyond the library catalog or beyond a group of libraries following the same cataloging rules.

Library catalog entries, as conceived in the era of book and card catalogs, were indivisible units, each one standing alone while functioning together within the catalog because of the consistency facilitated by the cataloging rules. The library catalog record is, in essence, a document, albeit a formalized and structured one.

The Singapore Framework represents a modular view of a domain of metadata. This model promotes a view of metadata as a network of data that can interact with any other community's data. The desire to be part of a broader information network through sharing, and not just sharing whole catalog records but linking data elements, requires that one's data must be structured as individual statements that can interact in a meaningful way.

FRBR arose out of a conscious need for just such a model. The IFLA study group was formed in 1991 shortly after the 1990 Stockholm Seminar on Cataloguing.[1] The group decided to develop an entity-relationship (ER) model. An ER model consists of entities ("things") that are the main components of the data to be created, the relationships between the entities, and the attributes of the entities. Motivating these choices in the FRBR model is a statement of user tasks that library metadata must address: find, identify, select, obtain.

The final version of the FRBR model was issued in 1998. Updated versions in 2008 and 2009 made minor changes but left the primary elements of FRBR intact.[2] Following the trend set by FRBR, IFLA groups are in the process of defining similar models for authority data (FRAD) and for subject authority data (FRSAR).[3] It is likely that more work will need to be done to integrate the three submodels into a single domain view.

*Singapore Framework for Dublin Core Application Profiles*
http://dublincore.org/documents/singapore-framework

## Entities and Relationships

The ER analysis of bibliographic data that FRBR provides does not differ conceptually from the information that has made up library cataloging for more than a century. What FRBR does, however, is make explicit the underlying structure of the bibliographic data. The entities are presented in three groups: Group 1 represents the resource being described and has four entities: work, expression, manifestation, and item; Group 2 represents agents that have relationships with the Group 1 entities: persons, corporate bodies, and families (see figure 8); and Group 3 represents entities with a topical relationship to the Group 1 entities. Group 3 adds four new entities—concept, object, place, and event—but it also includes all of the Group 1 and Group 2 entities since those can be the subjects of any resource being described.

The entities are the basic building blocks of the bibliographic domain: they are what the metadata must describe. The describing elements are called properties in Semantic Web terminology, but they are referred to in the FRBR model as attributes (see figure 9). The properties are what one usually thinks of as a data element. For example, the entity Person can have the properties *name, dates of birth and death, titles*, and other identifying information. The entity Work has *title of the work, form of the work*, and *date of the work*, among others.

The attributes describe the individual entities of the bibliographic description, but it is relationships between those attributes that have the potential for the creation of a rich knowledge network of bibliographic information. The great value of using entities and relationships is that they allow the creation of a network of connections that goes beyond the description of a single item, more accurately reflecting the rich interaction between the intellectual creations that are being cataloged. Most discussion of FRBR focuses on the three groups of entities (bibliographic description, agents, and subjects), yet about one third of the FRBR document is a description of the relationships that can exist between entities.

Bibliographic relationships have been recorded in library data to some extent, but only a few are manifested regularly in bibliographic products or systems. One familiar relationship is that of "cites" with its converse "is cited by." The Science Citation Index is entirely based on this key bibliographic relationship. Citation relationships are featured also in Google's Scholar product, and at least one community is experimenting with citation "types" using a citation ontology.[4]

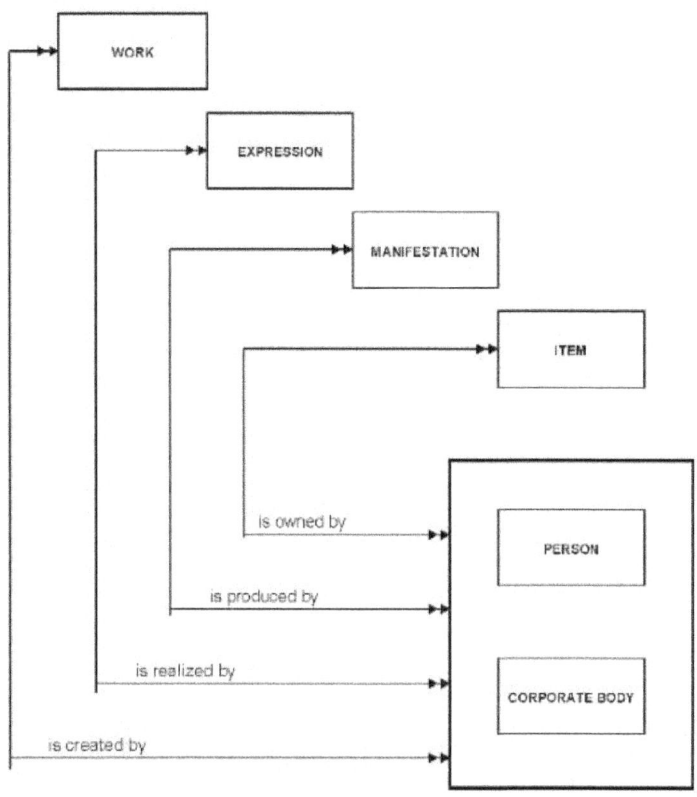

**Figure 8**
A sample diagram from the FRBR document showing the Group 2 data elements. Source: Robert L. Maxwell, *FRBR: A Guide for the Perplexed* (Chicago: American Library Association, 2007), p. 13.

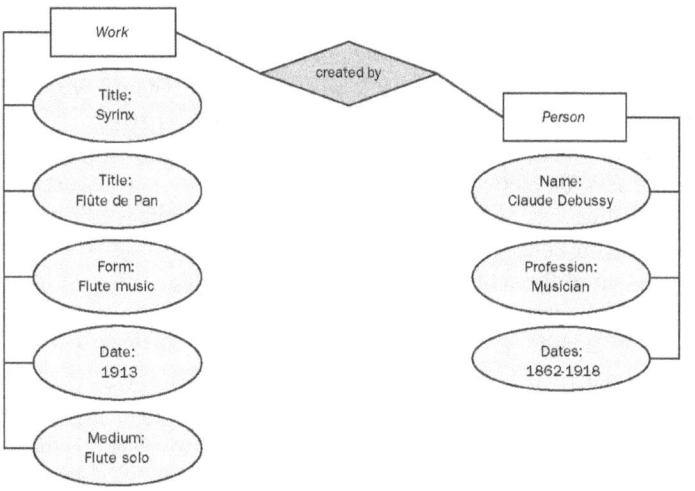

**Figure 9**
FRBR diagram showing attributes. Source: Robert L. Maxwell, *FRBR: A Guide for the Perplexed* (Chicago: American Library Association, 2007), p. 21.

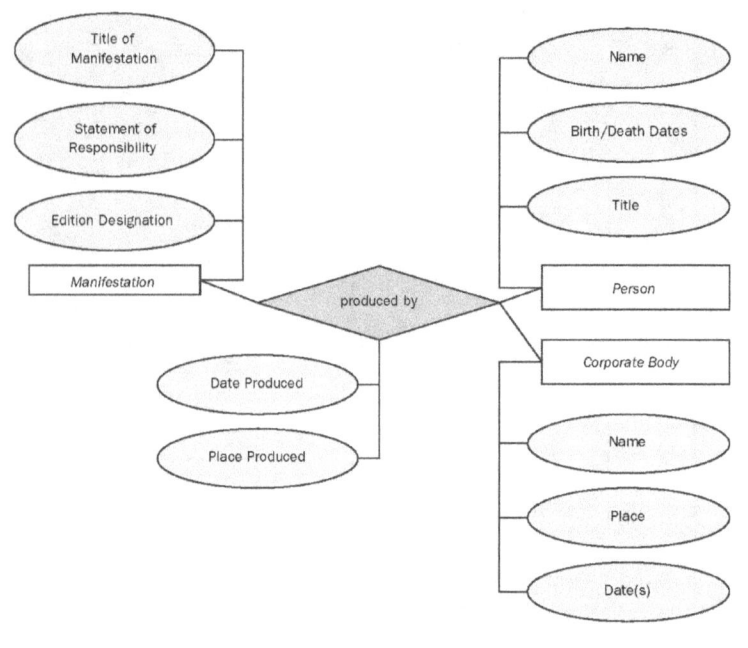

**Figure 10**
Source: Robert L. Maxwell, *FRBR: A Guide for the Perplexed* (Chicago: American Library Association, 2007), p. 9.

be noted in bibliographic records, but as nonspecific references in added entries or as notes intended solely for human readers. As part of an ER model, relationships are made explicit, as we will see further on.

Some of our misconceptions of FRBR may arise because of the starkness of the diagrams in the FRBR document. Visualization of abstract concepts is a fine art and can make all the difference in how or whether readers understand the ideas being presented. The diagrams in the FRBR document, while correct, are deceptive in their simplicity. Maxwell, in his book on FRBR, chooses to represent FRBR with an equally accurate but different choice of ER diagramming techniques. These diagrams may make FRBR clearer, as figure 10 shows.

This style of diagram makes it easier to see the relationships, and it also makes it easier to visualize a variety of cases. One aspect of FRBR as it is described and diagrammed is that it gives the impression of being a linear, hierarchical model from Work to Item. This is not the viewpoint of library cataloging, which has necessarily at its center a Manifestation. Without disturbing the meaning of FRBR, we can visualize it with the manifestation as the focus (see figure 11).

The user view of library data differs from that of the cataloger. Users seeking information on a topic could visualize the library's holdings as shown in figure 12.

It is possible that a library catalog could mimic this user view by presenting subjects as entities in the catalog, rather than as added entries on a bibliographic record. This approach is being experimented with on the Open Library, where subjects are treated as "first class" objects with their own Web pages (see figure 13).

Library records for serials often include previous and later titles assumed by the journal, and in some systems these records can be linked through their standard identifying numbers (usually ISSNs).

Many other relationships are inherent in bibliographic data but not usually presented in an actionable way. Tables of contents in a book are an example, where each entry represents a bibliographic unit that is in a part-whole relationship with the book, yet is not usually presented as a full bibliographic item.

Another example of a bibliographic relationship is pertinent to conceptual rather than structural relationships—that of the retelling of the same story, such as the relationship between Shakespeare's *Romeo and Juliet* and the modern urban rendition in *West Side Story*. These relationships are known and commonly analyzed in reviews and critical works, but bibliographic metadata has no vocabulary to express them. The relationships may

*Science Citation Index*
http://thomsonreuters.com/products_services/science/science_products/a-z/science_citation_index

*Google Scholar*
http://scholar.google.com

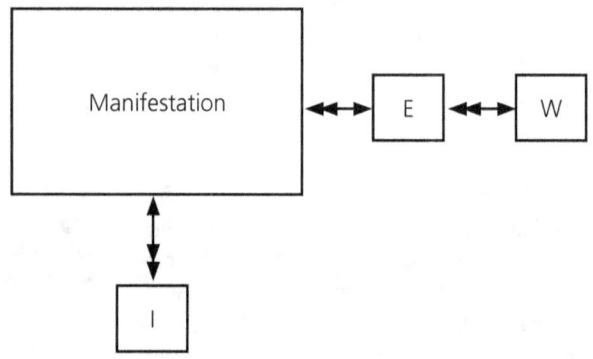

**Figure 11**
FRBR from a cataloger point of view.

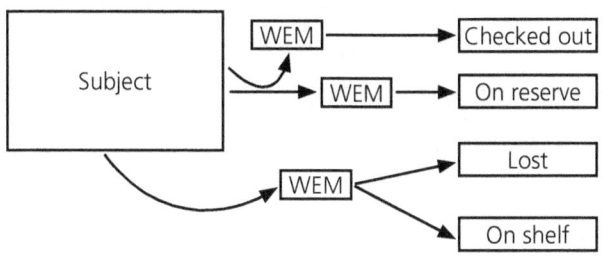

**Figure 12**
Possible view of FRBR entities from a user point of view.

*WorldCat Identities*
http://orlabs.oclc.org/Identities

*Wikipedia*
http://wikipedia.org

**Figure 13**
Screen shot from the Open Library webpage.

This is not unlike the treatment of persons in the WorldCat Identities pages, and both have some resemblance to what today's information seeker might expect to find at Wikipedia. Unlike Wikipedia, however, the Open Library display is generated on the fly from the bibliographic data in its database.

The FRBR entities lend themselves easily to different views of bibliographic data in a way that is less possible with the current "unit card" presentation of library data. The entity-relationship model promises a better solution than the "one view fits all" of the current bibliographic record.

## Beyond *R* Is for Record

Our current view of bibliographic data is that of catalog records that represent a manifestation (in FRBR terms) of a work. FRBR enforces this view with its very name, in which the final R is for *records*. There is a natural tendency to see FRBR as the model for a single bibliographic entity and conceive of the FRBR model as the description of a single bibliographic record. It would be more accurate to view FRBR as a model of a network of entities. Unfortunately, the FRBR document does not provide a view of this bibliographic network, perhaps in part because it is difficult to render in diagram form. Maxwell gives us a glimpse into this in his chapter on relationships. For example, figure 14 is Maxwell's diagram of a set of sequential relationships.

As you can see, rendering these relationships as diagrams is very complex. Yet it is these relationships that could transform library data into a true information network rather than a mere list of individual bibliographic items. No work actually stands alone in the human intellectual sphere; all precedents and influences either imitate previous works or stimulate the creation of new ones. This is what we could capture in a FRBR-ized bibliographic universe.

In today's bibliographic data, some relationships are inherent in the records that are created through the use of headings located in separate records:

Hamlet

Hamlet. 1798. Spanish

Hamlet [motion picture]

What FRBR allows us to do is to make manifest relationships that have been understated in bibliographic data in the past, and then provide the relationship information in a machine-actionable way (see figure 15).

In current cataloging, we must assume that our users are intelligent enough and have enough information to make the connections themselves through the text in the record. That may not always be the case, in part because

*Open Library*
http://openlibrary.org

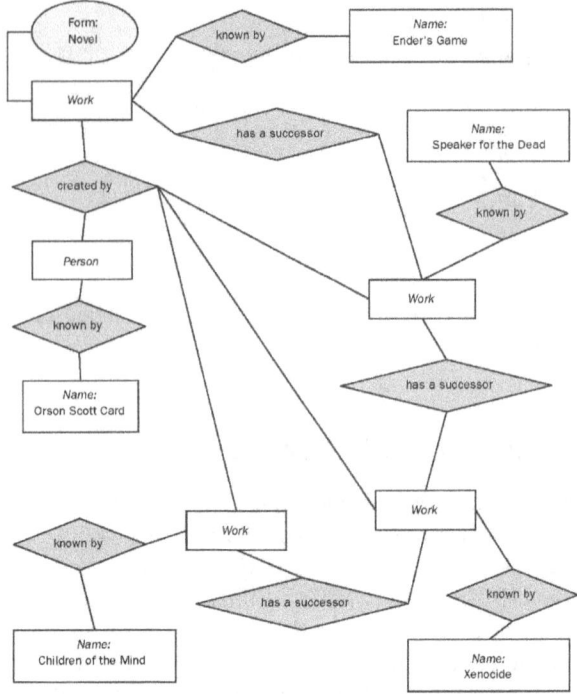

**Figure 14**
Some FRBR relationships. Source: Robert L. Maxwell, *FRBR: A Guide for the Perplexed* (Chicago: American Library Association, 2007), p. 104.

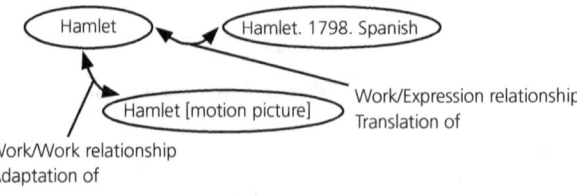

**Figure 15**
Explicit relationships in FRBR.

**The magnificent seven**

| | |
|---|---|
| Author: | John Sturges; William S Roberts; Yul Brynner; Steve McQueen; Eli Wallach; All authors |
| Publisher: | New York : MGM Home Entertainment Inc., 2001. |
| Series: | Western legends |
| Edition/Format: | DVD video : English : Special ed View all editions and formats |
| Summary: | The citizens of a small Mexican farming village hire seven gun fighters to defend them from a ruthless and exploitative group of bandits led by Calvera. As Calvera's next raid approaches, the peasants and the gun fighters work together to prepare to defend the village. |

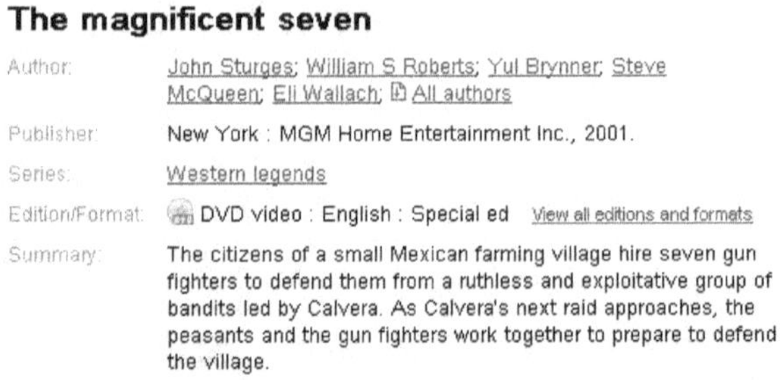

**Figure 16**
Default user view of item.

users may lack some background information needed, but often because they are unaware that the connecting information exists in the records or how to make use of it. The required information may not appear in the default view and may not be easy for the user to interpret (see figures 16 and 17).

Turning an informational note into a navigable relationship would allow systems to offer pathways between related bibliographic entities. There are many ways that these could be offered in systems, from simple links for "More" or "Related" to topic map styled graphs.

Not only could we gain this navigation capability within the library system, but the entities, relationships, and various attributes, freed from the confines of the bibliographic record, could begin to interact with data in other networks, including the mother of all networks, the World Wide Web.

## FRBR as Beta

While highly useful for any rethinking of library metadata practices, FRBR should not be seen as complete or perfected. Actual engagement with FRBR and attempts to use FRBR as a model are recent and not fully tested. There are criticisms that should be seriously studied. For example, Maxwell, in his book-length explication of FRBR, points out that FRBR's definition of the relationships of persons and corporate bodies to entities limited to "produce," thus excluding some relationships commonly recorded in archival and rare book cataloging, such as addressees and signers.[5] Svenonius finds the four user tasks to be incomplete and adds a fifth task, *navigate*.[6] Librarians specializing in serials and music materials have studied FRBR from their viewpoint and found some areas of difficulty in applying the model.[7] There is some debate on whether these reflect gaps in the model or in the understanding of the investigators.[8]

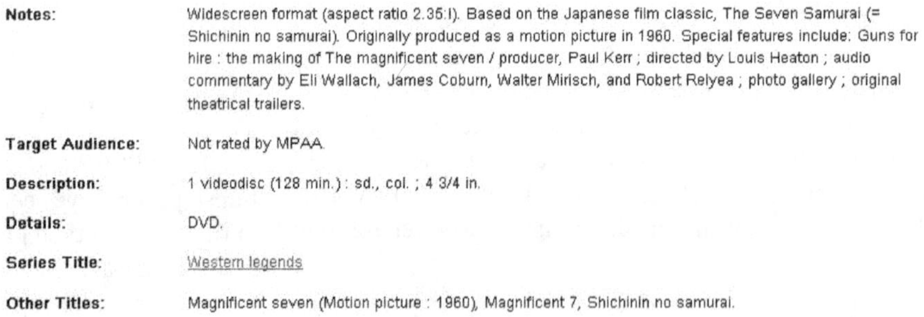

Information professionals who have attempted to cod-

| | |
|---|---|
| **Notes:** | Widescreen format (aspect ratio 2.35:1). Based on the Japanese film classic, The Seven Samurai (= Shichinin no samurai). Originally produced as a motion picture in 1960. Special features include: Guns for hire : the making of The magnificent seven / producer, Paul Kerr ; directed by Louis Heaton ; audio commentary by Eli Wallach, James Coburn, Walter Mirisch, and Robert Relyea ; photo gallery ; original theatrical trailers. |
| **Target Audience:** | Not rated by MPAA. |
| **Description:** | 1 videodisc (128 min.) : sd., col. ; 4 3/4 in. |
| **Details:** | DVD. |
| **Series Title:** | Western legends |
| **Other Titles:** | Magnificent seven (Motion picture : 1960), Magnificent 7, Shichinin no samurai. |

**Figure 17**
Information about relationships in detailed view.

ify FRBR for use in machine-readable metadata have found a different set of issues. There have been various RDF-based models of FRBR created, such as the "Expression of Core FRBR Concepts in RDF" and object-oriented FRBRoo created as part of the CIDOC Conceptual Reference Model. Both of these efforts found the need to add some entities in order to complete the model in RDF. The development of RDA in RDF also had reason to create a class for Agent that would encompass all of the Group 2 entities (person, corporate body, and family). These modifications do not mean that FRBR is fatally flawed; experimentation with FRBR in multiple environments is the best way to resolve any outstanding issues and provide a well-functioning domain model for future metadata development.

The most important benefit of a model like FRBR

*FRBRoo Introduction*
http://cidoc.ics.forth.gr/frbr_inro.html

is that it allows a focused discussion to take place. The model can and probably will be modified as the community gains more experience with it. It may even be modified to facilitate extracommunity communication about bibliographic items. An advantage of the ER model is that it can be extended to include additional entities and relationships, often without disrupting the existing ones. If one wants to add the relationships beyond *produce* that Maxwell mentions, that should be possible to do while leaving the existing structure alone.

When the Working Group on the Future of

*Expression of Core FRBR Concepts in RDF*
http://vocab.org/frbr/core.html

Bibliographic Control issued its report, *On the Record*, in early 2008, one of its recommendations was that work on the new cataloging rules, RDA, should be halted until more work could be done to exercise the concepts in FRBR and to further perfect that model.[9] RDA, however, is itself arguably the best test of the FRBR model because it makes use of FRBR as it was intended, as a model for library cataloging metadata. To make it possible to create metadata using RDA and FRBR, however, one first needs to define the elements of RDA in a machine-actionable format. That is precisely the goal of the RDA in RDF project, under the auspices of the Joint Steering Committee for RDA and the Dublin Core Metadata Initiative.

## Notes

1. Barbara B. Tillett, "IFLA Study on the Functional Requirements of Bibliographic Records: Theoretical and Practical Foundations" (paper presented at 60th IFLA General Conference, Havana, Cuba, Aug. 21-27, 1994)
2. IFLA Study Group on the Functional Requirements for Bibliographic Records, *Functional Requirements for Bibliographic Records: Final Report*, Sept. 1997, as amended and corrected through Feb. 2009, http://archive.ifla.org/VII/s13/frbr/frbr_2008.pdf (accessed Dec. 15, 2009),
3. Glenn E. Patton, ed. *Functional Requirements for Authority Data: A Conceptual Model* (Munich: K.G. Saur, 2009); "Functional Requirements for Subject Authority Records (FRSAR)," on hte IFLANET website, www.ifla.org/node/1297 (accessed Dec. 16, 2009).
4. David Shotton, "CiTO, the Citation Typing Ontology, and Its Use for Annotation of Reference Lists and Visualization of Citation Networks" (presentation, 12th annual Bio-Ontologies Meeting, Stockholm, Sweden, June 28, 2009). The ontology is available at http://purl.org/net/cito (accessed Dec. 17, 2009).
5. Robert L. Maxwell, *FRBR: A Guide for the Perplexed* (Chicago: American Library Association, 2007), 15.
6. Elaine Svenonius, *The Intellectual Foundation of Information Organization* (Cambridge, MA: MIT Press, 2000), 18.
7. "Variations/FRBR: Variations as a Testbed for the FRBR Conceptual Model," www.dlib.indiana.edu/projects/vfrbr (accessed Dec. 14, 2009); Kristin Antelman, "Identifying the Serial Work as a Bibliographic Entity," *Library Resources and Technical Services* 48, no. 4 (Oct. 2004): 238-255.
8. Barbara Tillett, letter to the editor, *Library Resources and Technical Services* 50, no. 3 (July 2006): 152-155 [a response to Ed Jones, "The FRBR Model as Applied to Continuing Resources," *Library Resources and Technical Services* 49, no .4 (Oct. 2005): 227-242].
9. *On the Record: Report of the Library of Congress Working Group on the Future of Bibliographic Control* (Washington, DC: Library of Congress, 2008).

# Chapter 4

# RDA in RDF

## Abstract

*The development of new cataloging rules that are based on the domain model provided by FRBR affords an opportunity to "data-fy" the underlying elements of the cataloging activity. In conjunction with members of the Dublin Core Metadata Initiative, the data elements identified in RDA have been defined using current Semantic Web standards. The elements now exist in an openly accessible registry on the Web where they can be downloaded and used by anyone wishing to describe bibliographic data. This work dovetails with similar efforts at the Library of Congress to define its key vocabularies in another Semantic Web format, SKOS. Together, these registered data elements can form the basis of a new generation of library data that can interact in the larger information space of linked data on the Web.*

There is a tendency today for different communities to create different metadata sets for similar, but not identical, needs. One has little choice when the metadata set, as defined, must be used as a whole or not at all. This is the case when the metadata is defined as a particular record structure, and the data elements are neither extendible nor reusable outside of that structure.

Once data elements are defined independently of a particular record standard, however, it becomes possible to create different applications using some of the same data elements. In theory, a bookstore and a library could use the same data elements where their interests are the same: title, publisher, year of publication. They could each also have different data elements for areas where they have different needs. Thus a library would have classification numbers and circulation information, while a bookstore would have shelf location and pricing (see figure 18).

It is only by defining our data elements independently of a record structure that this kind of sharing will become possible. In the Semantic Web world, the definition of data elements is the creation of an *ontology*, which is an expression of the vocabulary of a particular domain. It so happens that at the time that the creation of an ontology for library data started to be of interest to some in the library community, the community was also undergoing a major change in its approach to the creation of metadata, first because of FRBR, and next because of the development of RDA.[1] FRBR uses an entity-relation (ER) model for the description of the bibliographic domain of interest to libraries, and RDA consciously incorporates the FRBR entities and relationships into the cataloging rules. While a Semantic Web–based vocabulary could be created for the current cataloging rules, AACR2, there is an advantage to making this first effort with rules that have an explicit ER model as their basis.[2]

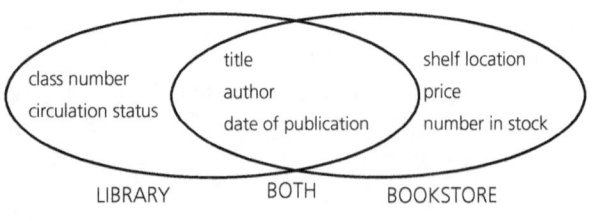

**Figure 18**
Overlap and differences in required metadata.

## RDA Background

The cataloging rules issued in a final draft in 2009 under the name Resource Description and Access (RDA) are the result of nearly ten years of study and are the culmination of nearly 150 years of thought about catalogs and cataloging. RDA is the first major revision of the rules governing library cataloging practices since the development of FRBR and was consciously aligned with the entity-relationship model of FRBR.

Like cataloging rules before it, RDA serves multiple functions. It is a set of rules that guide catalogers in the decisions that they must make in the course of creating a catalog entry. It is also implicitly a statement of the data elements that make up the bibliographic description. What RDA is *not* is as important as what it is. It is not a prescription for a machine-readable record format. RDA defines in some detail the strings that must be created to represent elements of the description, such as the recording of titles of works and the creation of access points. Although RDA states in its Prospectus that "it establishes a clear line of separation between the recording of data and the presentation of data,"[3] the descriptions and examples are recorded primarily as text strings. Some of those strings are necessarily of the nature of free text because they are transcriptions of data from the resource itself. Other strings may be entries from controlled vocabularies, including forms of names in authority-controlled entities such as the names of persons or corporate bodies.

RDA, as conceived by the Joint Steering Committee charged with its development, also includes a data element set. Each data element described in RDA is associated with one or more FRBR entities and has one or more possible value types. This is detailed in the element analysis of the final RDA draft.[4]

As a document, however, the elements are essentially inert; they exist on paper but not in a machine-actionable form. There is no direct path from the documentation to anything that could be used in a computer application.

A group of metadata developers active in the Dublin Core community recognized that RDA was on the threshold of making the transition from *conceptual* to *actionable* metadata. What it needed, though, was the creation of a machine-actionable ontology from the documented RDA data elements. In a meeting funded by ALA Publishing and held at the British Library on April 30 and May 1, 2007, representatives of DCMI met with members of the JSC and offered to collaborate on the creation of an RDF-compatible expression of the RDA element set, including the association with FRBR entities and relationships. This work was carried out by Metadata Management Associates and volunteers in the metadata community, with funding from the British Library and Siderean Software. The result is an online registry of RDA in RDF, the first definition of library cataloging data in a Semantic Web format.

## RDA in RDF

The definition of RDA in RDF uses three basic components: the FRBR entities (Groups 1, 2, and 3); the RDA-defined properties from the RDA element analysis, including the relationships between entities as defined in RDA; and the many lists of terms that are sprinkled throughout the RDA document itself. These latter are called "value vocabularies," using the Dublin Core Abstract Model terminology.

*Dublin Core Abstract Model*
http://dublincore.org/documents/abstract-model

### FRBR Entities

The FRBR entities serve as what RDF defines as *classes*. A class is a way to gather together like things so that we can say that both *Hamlet* and *Moby Dick* are members of the class Work, and "William Shakespeare" and "Herman Melville" are members of the class Person. Classes have particular attributes, known in RDF as *properties*. The properties of a Work, as defined by RDA, include a title and a form, while properties of a Person include name and dates of birth and death. In this way, the FRBR entities are the general organizing principle of the RDA element description.

### RDA Properties

Each data element defined by RDA is considered an RDF *property*. There are over 1,300 properties in the registered version of RDA, some of which are subproperties of other properties. The formal definition of a property follows conventions established in the Semantic Web world, including the extensions developed by the Dublin Core community.

*British Library*
www.bl.uk

*Siderean Software*
www.siderean.com

*Registry of RDA in RDF*
http://metadataregistry.org/rdabrowse.htm

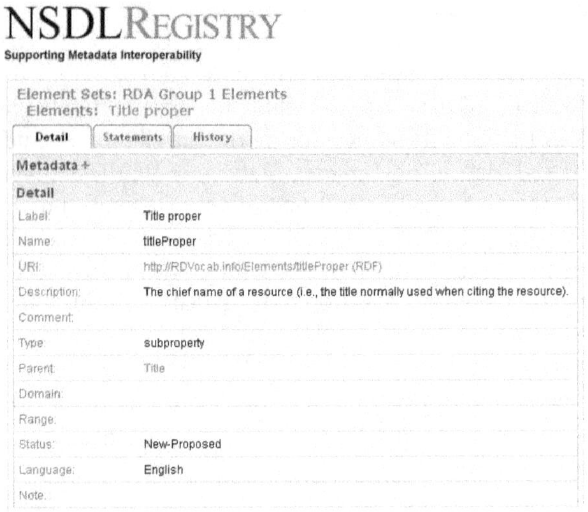

**Figure 19**
Overview of a property.

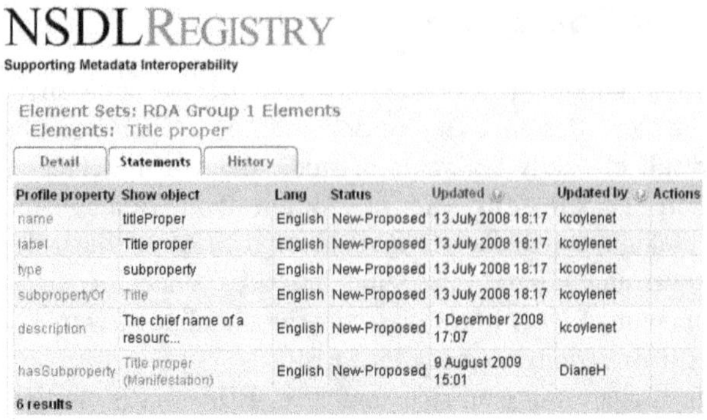

**Figure 20**
Statement view of a property.

The high number of elements is due in part to the need by the developers of RDA to have a specific entry for each element with its pairing to a FRBR Group1 entity. It is this paired element that connects directly to the text of RDA and to the list of elements and definitions in the RDA documentation. The registrars chose to encode an entry for an element independent of its FRBR entity and an entry (or entries in the case of elements that can be associated with more than one FRBR entity) for the element and its associated FRBR entity to allow for extensibility. Registered properties are available online in a human-readable display with both an overview and a display of statements (see figures 19 and 20).

When accessed by a program rather than a browser, the registry entry is returned in a machine-readable format—RDF/XML in the case shown in figure 21.

The same registry data serves machine-processing needs as well as a useful display for metadata creators and any metadata applications that have user-oriented displays. It is not necessary to maintain two separate versions of the same information in order to serve both human users and programmatic needs.

The elements of the registry entry for properties are as follows:

- Identifier (URI)—a Semantic Web–compatible identifier that begins with "http://rdvocab.info/" identifying each term.
- Name—a machine-friendly form of the name of the element, generally in "camel case": titleProper.
- Label—a human-display label for the element: "Title proper." Labels are language-specific. RDA provides labels in English, but labels can be added in any language.
- Description—a human-readable definition of the element or term. The descriptions in the registry are those supplied in the RDA Glossary. For example, the description for Title proper is "The chief name of a resource (i.e., the title normally used when citing the resource)." Like labels, descriptions are language-specific, and others could be added in other languages.
- Domain—the class or classes to which the element belongs. The class is the FRBR entity with which the property is associated: "FRBR Manifestation." Each element is entered into the registry in two forms: one that specifies the domain as defined in RDA, and one that presents the element without a domain designation. This latter can then be used by communities not adhering to FRBR or by those who wish to make a different decision in terms of the binding of elements to FRBR classes.
- Range—the value types that can be input as the element contents. Because RDA generally allows both controlled and uncontrolled values, this will be defined most often in the application profile rather than in the element definition.
- Type—the type of element, either property or subproperty, class or subclass.
- subPropertyOf—for properties that have a hierarchically superordinate property, such as "Variant title," which is a subproperty of "Title."
- hasSubproperty—For properties with subproperties associated with them, all subproperties are linked to the registry entry for the property. For example, the property "Title" has subproperties "Title proper," "Key title," and "Abbreviated title," among others.

It may seem counterintuitive, but the relationships between FRBR entities are also coded as properties, as

*RDA Glossary*
www.rdaonline.org/constituencyreview/Phase1Gloss_10_21_08.pdf

```xml
<?xml version="1.0" encoding="UTF-8"?>
<rdf:RDF xmlns="http://www.w3.org/1999/02/22-rdf-syntax-ns#"
xml:base="http://RDVocab.info/Elements"
xmlns:rdf="http://www.w3.org/1999/02/22-rdf-syntax-ns#"
xmlns:rdfs="http://www.w3.org/2000/01/rdf-schema#"
xmlns:skos="http://www.w3.org/2004/02/skos/core#"
xmlns:dc="http://purl.org/dc/elements/1.1/"
xmlns:dct="http://purl.org/dc/terms/"
xmlns:owl="http://www.w3.org/2002/07/owl#"
xmlns:foaf="http://xmlns.com/foaf/0.1/"
xmlns:reg="http://metadataregistry.org/uri/profile/RegAp/">
<!-- Element Set: RDA Group 1 Elements -->
<rdf:Description rdf:about="http://RDVocab.info/Elements">
<dc:title xml:lang="en">RDA Group 1 Elements</dc:title>
<skos:note  xml:lang="en">This is the provisional registration of the RDA
Group 1 Element Vocabulary, managed by the DCMI/RDA Task Group.</skos:note>
<foaf:homepage rdf:resource="http://dublincore.org/dcmirdataskgroup/"/>
</rdf:Description>
<!--Property: Title proper-->
<rdf:Description rdf:about="http://RDVocab.info/Elements/titleProper">
<rdfs:isDefinedBy rdf:resource="http://RDVocab.info/Elements" />
<reg:status rdf:resource="http://metadataregistry.org/uri/RegStatus/1002" />
<reg:name xml:lang="en">titleProper</reg:name>
<rdfs:label xml:lang="en">Title proper</rdfs:label>
<rdf:type rdf:resource="http://www.w3.org/1999/02/22-rdf-syntax-ns#Property"
/>
<skos:definition xml:lang="en">The chief name of a resource (i.e., the title
normally used when citing the resource).</skos:definition>
</rdf:Description>
<!-- Status properties used in this document  -->
<skos:Concept rdf:about="http://metadataregistry.org/uri/RegStatus/1002">
       <skos:prefLabel xml:lang="en">New-Proposed</skos:prefLabel>
</skos:Concept>
</rdf:RDF>
```

**Figure 21**
Registry entry in machine-readable format.

---

are the creator and contributor roles. This is an appropriate treatment of relationships in RDF, where all statements are reduced to the subject-predicate-object form (see figure 22).

Each of the properties would actually be represented by a URI in a machine-readable triple. This would look something like the diagram in figure 23.

In figure 23, the persons are identified using the identifier for the Library of Congress Name Authority record (although this form of the LCNA is not yet available on the id.loc.gov site). The book is identified using its LC Catalog Number in a standard format provided by LC. This number identifies the manifestation, not the Work, so this illustration is not quite accurate from a strict FRBR point of view, but it satisfies RDF requirements. The relationship property uses the identifiers from the RDA Registry for author and illustrator. As ungainly as the diagram is in this form, this is the preferred way to represent data for applications using Semantic Web technology. Human users of the data should not have to interact with this view, and the data could readily be displayed in any one of many familiar formats:

1.

Through the looking-glass, and what Alice found there

By Lewis Carroll

Illustrated by John Tenniel

2.

Title: Through the looking-glass, and what Alice found there

Author: Carroll, Lewis

Illustrator: Tenniel, John

Relationships can be between any entities, such as between Works, between Expressions, or between Persons. These, too, are defined in the registry as properties and can be used in RDF-compatible statements. Figure 24 shows a triple that states that the 1933 film *Alice in Wonderland* was based on the book *Through the Looking-Glass*. The permalink from OCLC WorldCat is used in this case to identify the film.

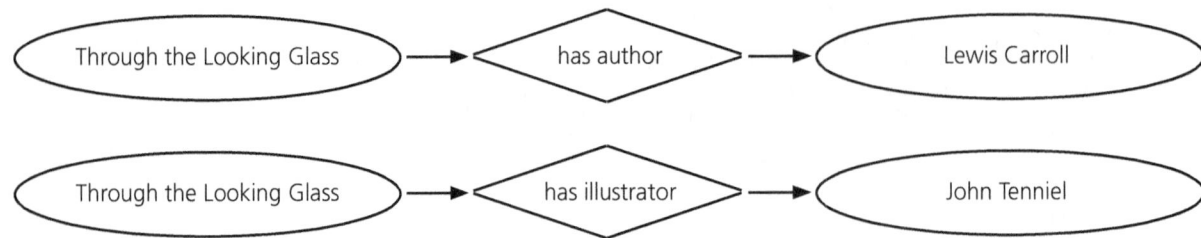

**Figure 22**
An author and a contributor, in triple form.

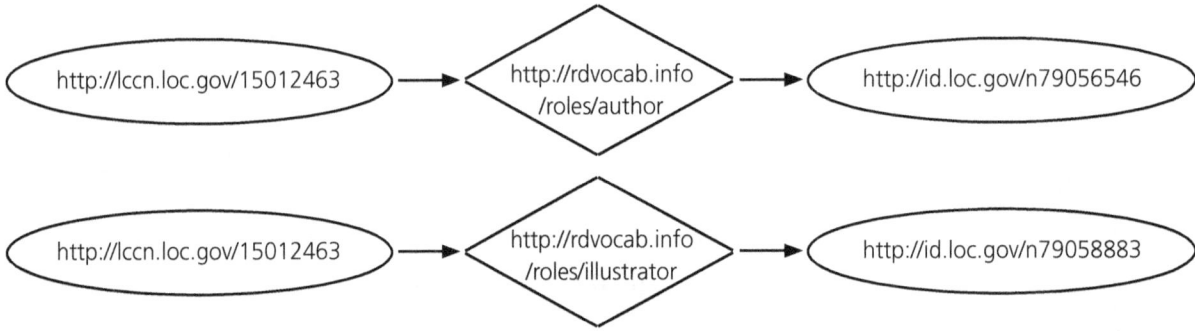

**Figure 23**
An author and a contributor represented by URIs.

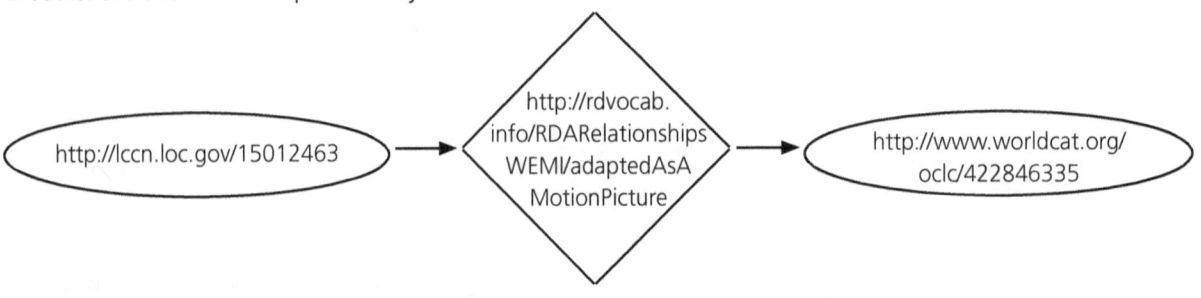

**Figure 24**
A work/work relationship between the book and the motion picture.

### RDA Value Vocabularies

There are numerous areas in the instructions in the text of RDA where the cataloguer is instructed to make a selection from a limited list of values. These controlled lists are called *vocabularies* in the registry and often referred to as *value vocabularies* in Dublin Core documentation because entries in these lists are used as the value of a property. For example, one would say that the value of a particular instance of RDA Content type is "text," which is taken from the list of content types defined in RDA. When the value does not come from a value vocabulary, it is simply a character string. When it does comes from a value vocabulary and that vocabulary itself has been defined in RDF, the value then has a unique identifier, in this case "http://RDVocab.info/termList/RDAContentType/1020," which is the URI for the RDA Content Type "text."

The value vocabularies are defined using the Simple Knowledge Organization System, SKOS, which is an RDF-compliant language specifically designed for term lists and thesauri. As mentioned in chapter 2, SKOS permits the creation of a group of concepts with relationships, such as broader and narrower concepts. Many of the vocabularies in RDA are simple lists of terms, but SKOS allows for the presentation of both preferred and alternate display and entry vocabularies, as well as human-readable definitions of the terms. SKOS can be used to provide vocabularies in more than one language.

An example of a simple list is that for *RDA base material*. This is a list of terms with no broader or narrower relationships (see figure 25).

**Figure 25**
The registered vocabulary for RDA Base Material.

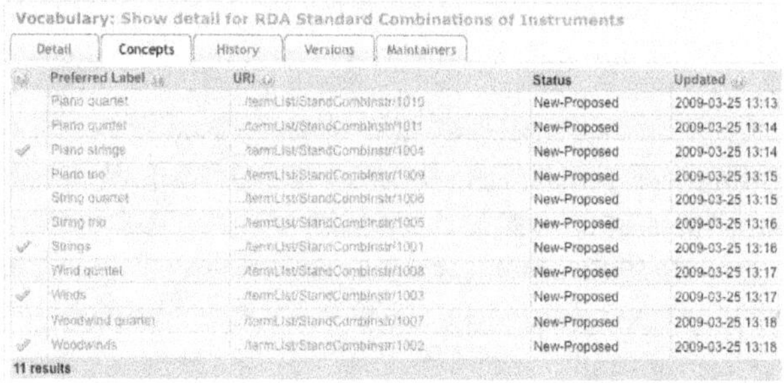

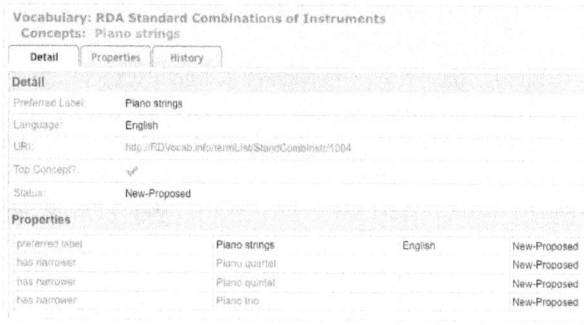

**Figure 27**
A detailed view of the term "Piano strings" showing related narrower terms.

**Figure 28**
A view of the term "Piano quintet" with a reference to broader term "Piano strings."

**Figure 26**
The registered vocabulary for RDA Standard Combinations of Instruments showing top level terms.

The vocabulary *RDA standard combinations of instruments* does have structure. The top level terms in that structure are noted in figure 26 with a check mark.

The detailed view of a top-level term shows the narrower terms (see figure 27).

Reciprocally, the narrower term's entry records the relationship with the top level term (see figure 28).

RDA defines nearly seventy such vocabulary lists, but this is not by any means an exhaustive treatment of the vocabularies that may be used in bibliographic records. The Library of Congress is working to provide the bibliographic vocabularies under its control in Semantic Web–compatible formats,[5] and the National Library of Medicine has available a version of MeSH in SKOS format.[6] In addition, the library community will make use of standard lists defined by authoritative organizations like the International Standards Organization. Specialist communities from medicine and law to art and architecture often have term lists specific to their interests. Many of these are not yet available in a Semantic Web format, but the trend to provide this data for reuse in Semantic Web environments is beginning.

## Maintenance of the Metadata Standard

One of the big issues for any standard is that of maintenance. Maintenance means either constant or periodic revision of the standard to make sure it keeps up to date with the needs of its users. The maintenance activity must also engage the community in decision making and inform all relevant parties of proposed changes and timelines. In the past, the library community has been hindered by very slow update cycles for its standards. Updates to cataloging rules have been years, and even decades, apart, making it impossible for library data creation to keep pace with the rapid evolution of information resources. Bulletins were issued in the time periods between major revisions, but systems were slow to make changes, in part because changes were almost always disruptive in nature.

The definition of elements and vocabularies in a machine-actionable format has the potential to make maintenance of the elements of the cataloging standard easier, faster, and more visible to the community. It also

*RDA/MARC Working Group of the Joint Steering Committee for the Development of RDA*
www.rda-jsc.org/rdamarcwg.html

could facilitate the update of systems that use the elements and vocabularies.

In the past it was necessary to modify the cataloging standard in order to add new elements or vocabulary terms. This was also true of the standard machine-readable record used by library systems, MARC21. The lengthy process to add a new vocabulary entry to the standard has meant that often years could pass between an initial proposal and the approval of a change. Minor changes, such as adding a new value to an established term list, would go through the same process as major changes, such as adding or modifying significant data elements.

The metadata registry holding the RDA vocabularies has been designed to allow terms and elements to be added on a provisional basis for the purposes of development and testing. Provisional terms are marked so they could be selected for use by systems developers only when they are prepared to perform tests. Having provisional entry of new terms in the standard registry also allows for the time needed for upgrades to user interfaces and training materials.

Note that each value vocabulary could be maintained separately, and changes to one list do not affect other lists or the defined properties. Potentially, maintenance of specialist lists, such as those for music, film, or government documents, could be assigned to the interested community to manage.

With elements and vocabularies in a downloadable machine-readable format, systems can receive changes on a schedule or on an ad hoc basis, as desired. Registry entries can contain the display forms and definitions that will be needed for cataloging functions and used in the user interface so all of the information needed to incorporate a new term into an application is readily available in one place.

Version control is a key element of standards maintenance, and each entry in the registry is given a version stamp. Older versions can be retained, much like older forms of entries are retained commonly in wikis. This allows users to see how a term has changed over time—a feature that is missing in today's standards and one that makes the combination of current records and older files of records extremely difficult.

## RDA Vocabularies and the Bibliographic Record

The purpose of creating RDF-defined vocabularies is to establish compatibility between applications at a data level rather than at a record level. Among the advantages of well-defined metadata elements is that metadata from different sources and residing in different records can be compatible, even if the record formats themselves are not.

Linked data relies on data in a statement-level format, the *triple*, which serves as a universal microformat that nearly all Semantic Web–compatible applications should be able to provide.

How the data elements are combined into a record format is still up for discussion. The MARC21 community is investigating to what extent RDA can be expressed in that existing format, but it seems clear that the full flexibility and extensibility of RDA goes beyond what can be done in a record format that is already experiencing difficulties in keeping up with needed changes.

There are some (probably valid) assumptions that RDA will be expressed in an XML format. How this will be structured is not known. The eXtensible Catalog project (XC) provides an example of RDF-compliant and FRBR-compliant records. The record examples in figures 29 and 30, received via correspondence with J. Bowen, use only a few RDA vocabulary elements to fill in where Dublin Core, which forms the basis of the XC metadata, is lacking. While not fully expressive of RDA, the XC metadata record does make use of the FRBR Group 1 entities in its record structure, creating separate records for each Group 1 entity, such as these two records for a Work and an Expression.

Note that each of the described entities has a unique identifier and that the two records are linked through the statement in the expression record:

```
<xc:workExpressed>oai:mst.
rochester.edu:MST/
MARCToXCTransformation/10081</
xc:workExpressed>
```

Schematically, this could be diagrammed as a standard RDF triple (see figure 31).

If one wishes to participate in the linked data community, then the data must be expressed as triples rather than XML records. Triples may represent the same data as an XML record, but they don't constitute a record per se. Triples form a linked set of data that has no defined boundaries. Triples are hard to show because they are not very human-readable. I present them in a somewhat schematic way in figure 32, but remember that each property is either a character string (shown here in quotes) or a URI in URL format.

This "triple" form of RDF statements is awkward from a human standpoint because each statement contains only one relationship. Natural language expresses the same information in a much more compact form, such as "Akira Kurosawa was the director of *Shichinin no samurai* (also known as the *Seven Samurai*), which was adapted as *The Magnificent 7*." However, the triples logically form a kind of machine-readable sentence, as shown in figure 33.

Both the XML record format and the RDF triple for-

```xml
<xc:frbr xmlns:xc="http://www.extensiblecatalog.info/Elements"
xmlns:xsi="http://www.w3.org/2001/XMLSchema-instance"
xmlns:rdvocab="http://rdvocab.info/Elements"
xmlns:dcterms="http://purl.org/dc/terms/"
xmlns:rdarole="http://rdvocab.info/roles">
<xc:entity type="work"
id="oai:mst.rochester.edu:MST/MARCToXCTransformation/10081">
    <dcterms:subject xsi:type="dcterms:LCC">PS3505.U334</dcterms:subject>
    <dcterms:subject xsi:type="dcterms:DDC">811/.52</dcterms:subject>
    <dcterms:subject xsi:type="dcterms:DDC">B</dcterms:subject>
    <rdarole:author>Sawyer-Lauc<U+0327>anno, Christopher, 1951-
</rdarole:author>
    <rdvocab:titleOfWork>E.E. Cummings :</rdvocab:titleOfWork>
    <xc:subject xsi:type="dcterms:LCSH">Cummings, E. E. (Edward Estlin),
1894-1962.</xc:subject>
    <xc:subject xsi:type="dcterms:LCSH">Poets, American-20th century-
Biography.</xc:subject>
</xc:entity>
</xc:frbr>
```

**Figure 29**
XC XML record for a Work.

```xml
<?xml version="1.0" encoding="UTF-8"?>
<xc:frbr xmlns:xc="http://www.extensiblecatalog.info/Elements"
xmlns:xsi="http://www.w3.org/2001/XMLSchema-instance"
xmlns:rdvocab="http://rdvocab.info/Elements"
xmlns:dcterms="http://purl.org/dc/terms/"
xmlns:rdarole="http://rdvocab.info/roles">
<xc:entity type="expression"
id="oai:mst.rochester.edu:MST/MARCToXCTransformation/10082">
    <xc:titleOfExpression>E.E. Cummings :</xc:titleOfExpression>
    <rdvocab:illustrationContent>ill. ;</rdvocab:illustrationContent>
    <xc:workExpressed>oai:mst.rochester.edu:MST/MARCToXCTransformation/1008
1</xc:workExpressed>
</xc:entity>
</xc:frbr>
<?xml version="1.0" encoding="UTF-8"?>
```

**Figure 30**
XC XML record for an Expression.

mat of data are valid to use. The record format creates a kind of container that can keep one set of data elements together for an application's purposes. The triple format allows the individual statements within the data to interact with other statements and form a constantly growing web of information.

One of the big questions relating to the creation of RDF data is how identifiers will be created for all of the metadata instances created in libraries. In some ideal universe where everything is perfectly neat—obviously not the one we occupy—there would be a single, universal identifier for each Work, each Person, each Place, and so on. This is unlikely to happen, although any sharing of identifiers increases the interoperability of data. The reality will undoubtedly be that, as in the examples above, some if not all of the identifiers assigned will be only locally meaningful. There could be aggregation services that perform a similar matching that OCLC provides for library MARC records, bringing together data from different systems and associating that data with a shared identity. For this, the bibliographic data itself will be used, as it is today, to infer that two separately created bibliographic descriptions are describing the same bibliographic resource.

With data in a Web-compatible format, there is also the possibility of creating Web-based data-creation tools, with broad sharing of identified elements such as Works, Persons, and Places as well as relationships. The more that identifiers are shared, the more accurate any state-

**Figure 31**
RDF triple of the Expression-to-Work relationships.

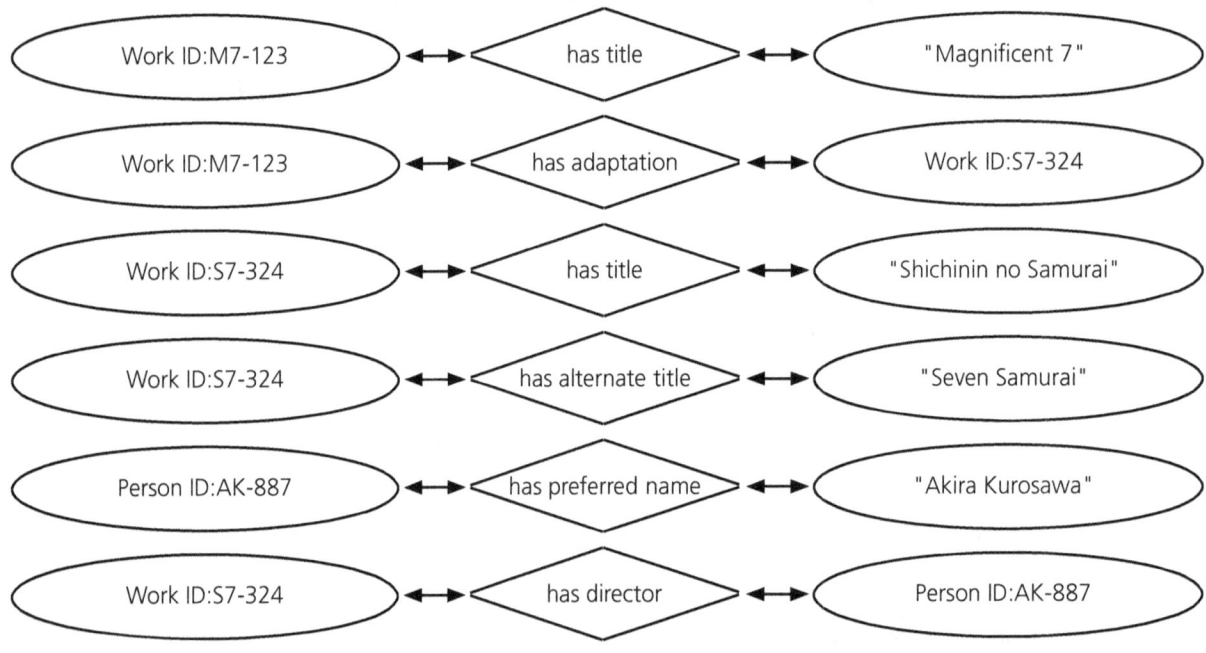

**Figure 32**
Complex set of triples about "Magnificent 7."

ment that "A is the same as B" can be, whether that is for a Work, a Person, a Place, or any other instance of an entity or property.

## Application Profiles

The over six hundred pages of the *Anglo-American Cataloguing Rules* (2nd edition) and the many hundreds of properties defined for the new cataloging rules, Resource Description and Access (RDA), are all the proof we need that the library cataloging rules attempt to cover the widest possible range of cataloging situations. Perhaps only the largest and most varied of libraries will have a need for all of the rules and data elements, and in fact, studies of MARC data show that the majority of data elements defined in that standard are seldom used out of a body of millions of cataloging examples.[7]

Libraries often find a need to create custom versions of the cataloging rules that are tailored to their specific needs. The RDA Online product being prepared by the publishing office of the American Library Association includes a customization function called "workflows" precisely because of this need. These workflows allow one to select from the RDA chapters and sections that are pertinent to the library's cataloging activity.

The information technology world has a similar concept for the customization of applications call "application profiles" (APs). Application profiles are a selection of data elements from a larger universe. The Dublin Core Metadata Initiative has developed an RDF-compliant, machine-readable expression of application profiles. Called the Dublin Core Description Set Profile (DSP), it provides a standard format that facilitates the creation of applications from the selected data elements.[8] The AP consists of a selection of RDF-compliant elements, and a definition of constraints related to those properties. Constraints consist of the declaration of repeatability, whether the elements are mandatory or optional, and any requirements for the types of values the elements will allow (plain text, controlled vocabularies, and so on).[9]

In an RDF-compliant application profile, elements and vocabularies can be taken from any suitable defined

*eXtensible Catalog: Metadata*
www.extensiblecatalog.org/Metadata

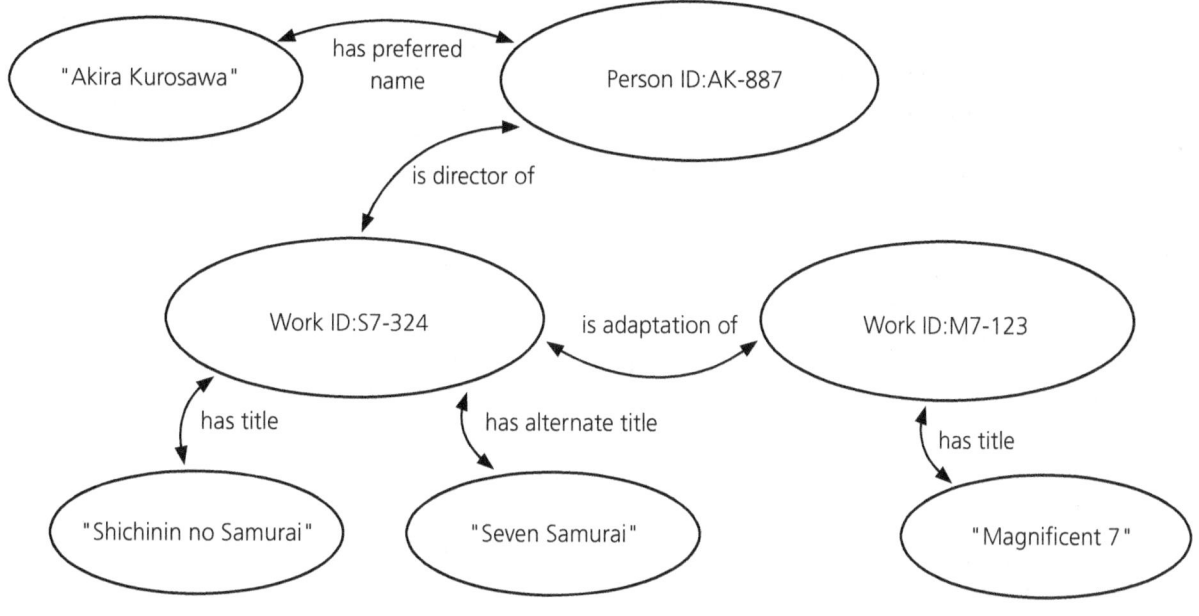

**Figure 33**
"Akira Kurosawa was the director of *Shichinin no samurai* (also known as the *Seven Samurai*), which was adapted as *The Magnificent 7.*"

set, and many Semantic Web applications work with a mix of elements from numerous sources. There is a conscious effort in that community to reuse rather than reinvent as part of the goal of interoperability over the entire Web. An application profile would therefore describe the particular mix of elements that had been chosen for a particular application.

Library community members could create any number of application profiles to meet their needs. There could be profiles for specialist communities, like visual resources or law collections. There could be profiles based on the languages of the collection that don't include rules for languages not needed. There could be simplified rules for minimal cataloging. The key, however, is that all of these customized profiles would be compatible with each other because they all would make use of the same defined and registered metadata properties. Undoubtedly some core properties will be used by all or at least most of the profiles, while other, more specialized properties will be needed only by a few members of the community.

*RDA Online*
http://rdaonline.org

While RDA intends to be as complete a set of metadata as possible, the adoption of application profiles would allow any community that wishes to use RDA to extend the vocabulary for local or specialist needs. It would no longer be necessary to entirely recreate a metadata set if RDA is found to only partially fulfill an institution's needs. Application profiles are the technical mechanism that support the data sharing that was introduced at the beginning of this chapter (see figure 34).

## A Word about the Future

RDF is not a magic spell that will make library data perfect. It is today's technology wave, arising out of the current capabilities of networked information resources. It will, somewhere down the line, be replaced by another technology. Where RDF differs most from the present system of bibliographic records is in allowing bibliographic descriptions to interact, extend, and influence each other and to interact at a statement level with other data from

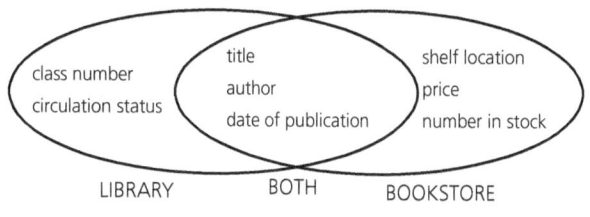

**Figure 34**
In application profiles, differences are accommodated with disrupting the advantages of shared data.

library and nonlibrary sources. The advantages to the library community are unmistakable.

It may be useful here to remember that when the MARC record was first developed, it was intended solely as a better way to issue printed card sets from the Library of Congress. Yet the machine-readable format made possible the creation of online catalogs, something that previously had been unthinkable. We cannot know today what innovations could be fostered through the transformation of library data to a new technology, but the possibilities are intriguing, not so much for how this could change the act of cataloging but for the new user services that could be built with a more flexible data carrier.

## Notes

1. IFLA Study Group on the Functional Requirements for Bibliographic Records, *Functional Requirements for Bibliographic Records: Final Report*, Sept. 1997, as amended and corrected through Feb. 2009, http://archive.ifla.org/VII/s13/frbr/frbr_2008.pdf (accessed Dec. 14, 2009); Joint Steering Committee for Development of RDA, "RDA: Resource Description and Access," www.rda-jsc.org/rda.html (accessed Dec. 14, 2009).
2. American Library Association, *Anglo-American Cataloguing Rules*, 2nd ed. (London: Library Association, 1978).
3. "RDA–Resource Description and Access: A Prospectus," rev. 7, July 1, 2009, p. 2, Joint Steering Committee for the Development of RDA website, www.rda-jsc.org/docs/5rda-prospectusrev7.pdf (accessed Dec. 18, 2009).
4. "RDA Element Analysis," rev. 2, Oct. 26, 2008, Joint Steering Committee for the Development of RDA website, www.rda-jsc.org/docs/5rda-elementanalysisrev2.pdf (accessed Dec. 14, 2009).
5. See "Authorities and Vocabularies" on the Library of Congress website, http://id.loc.gov/authorities.
6. "Neurocommons Alpha" is available online to those with a username and password at http://sw.neurocommons.org/2007/kb-sources/medline/medline-mesh.tgz.
7. MARC Content Designation Utilization: Inquiry and Analysis blog, www.mcdu.unt.edu (accessed Dec. 14, 2009).
8. Mikael Nilsson, "Description Set Profiles: A Constraint Language for Dublin Core Application Profiles," March 31, 2008, http://dublincore.org/documents/2008/03/31/dc-dsp (accessed Dec. 14, 2009).
9. Karen Coyle and Thomas Baker, "Guidelines for Dublin Core Application Profiles," May 18, 2009, http://dublincore.org/documents/profile-guidelines (accessed Dec. 14, 2009).

---

## Metadata Models of the World Wide Web, continued from page 19

### Notes

1. Tim Berners-Lee, James Hendler, and Ora Lassila, "The Semantic Web," *Scientific American*, May 2001: 34–43.
2. Tim Berners-Lee, "Linked Data," July 27, 2006, last updated June 18, 2009, World Wide Web Consortium (W3C) website, www.w3.org/DesignIssues/LinkedData.html (accessed Dec. 16, 2009).
3. "DCMI Metadata Terms," Jan. 14, 2008, on the Dublin Core Metadata Initiative website, http://dublincore.org/documents/dcmi-terms (accessed Dec. 16, 2009)
4. Mikael Nilsson, Thomas Baker, and Pete Johnston, "The Singapore Framework for Dublin Core Application Profiles," Jan. 14, 2008, on the Dublin Core Metadata Initiative website, http://dublincore.org/documents/singapore-framework (accessed Dec. 16, 2009).

# Resources

## FRBR

### Official Documents at IFLA

IFLA Study Group on the Functional Requirements for Bibliographic Records. *Functional Requirements for Bibliographic Records: Final Report*, Sept. 1997, as amended and corrected through Feb. 2009, http://archive.ifla.org/VII/s13/frbr/frbr_2008.pdf.

"FRBR Bibliography." Last updated Oct. 27, 2009. www.ifla.org/en/node/881.

IFLA's FRBR Review Group Discussion List. http://infoserv.inist.fr/wwsympa.fcgi/info/frbr.

Patton, Glenn E., ed. *Functional Requirements for Authority Data: A Conceptual Model.* IFLA Series on Bibliographic Control 34. Munich: K.G. Saur, 2009.

### Analysis of FRBR

Carlyle, Allyson. "Understanding FRBR as a Conceptual Model: FRBR and the Bibliographic Universe." *Library Resources and Technical Services* 50, no. 4 (Oct. 2006): 264–273.

Le Bœuf, Patrick. *Functional Requirements for Bibliographic Records (FRBR): Hype or Cure-all?* Binghamton, NY: Haworth Information Press, 2005.

Maxwell, Robert L. *FRBR: A Guide for the Perplexed.* Chicago: American Library Association, 2008.

Miksa, Shawne. "Understanding 'Support' of FRBR's Four User Tasks in MARC Encoded Bibliographic Records." *ASIST Bulletin* 33, no. 6 (Sept. 2007): 24–26.

Tillett, Barbara. *What Is FRBR? A Conceptual Model for the Bibliographic Universe.* Washington, DC: Library of Congress Cataloging Distribution Service, 2003.

Yee, Martha M. "FRBR and Moving Image Materials: Content (Work and Expression) versus Carrier (Manifestation)." In *Understanding FRBR: What It Is and How It Will Affect Our Retrieval Tools*, edited by Arlene G. Taylor., 117–130. Westport, CT: Greenwood Publishing, 2007. Retrieved from http://escholarship.org/uc/item/60t54503.

### FRBR Tests and Implementations

Davis, Ian, and Richard Newman, with Bruce D'Arcus. "Expression of Core FRBR Concepts in RDF." 2005, updated 2009. http://vocab.org/frbr/core.html.

Doerr, Martin and Patrick LeBœuf, eds. *FRBR Object-Oriented Definition and Mapping to FRBR-ER* (version 0.8.1). May 2007. http://cidoc.ics.forth.gr/docs/frbr_oo/frbr_docs/FRBR_oo_V0.8.1c.pdf.

eXtensible Catalog Project, Metadata Standards and Schema. www.extensiblecatalog.org/technology/metadata.

Indiana University. "Variations/FRBR: Variations as a Testbed for the FRBR Conceptual Model." www.dlib.indiana.edu/projects/vfrbr.

Joint Information Systems Committee (JISC). "Scholarly Works Application Profile (SWAP)." On the JISC Digital Repository Wiki. www.ukoln.ac.uk/repositories/digirep/index/Eprints_Application_Profile.

## OCLC Research

FRBR Activities Page. www.oclc.org/research/activities/past/orprojects/frbr.

FictionFinder. www.oclc.org/research/activities/fictionfinder

Work Records in WorldCat. www.oclc.org/research/activities/workrecs.

xISBN (Web service). www.worldcat.org/affiliate/webservices/xisbn/app.jsp.

VTLS. FRBR Software as a Service. www.vtls.com.

## RDA

### Official Documents

Joint Steering Committee for Development of RDA. www.rda-jsc.org.

RDA-L Discussion List. www.rda-jsc.org/rdadiscuss.html.

### RDA Online

RDA Online. http://rdaonline.org.

### Registry of RDA Vocabularies

National Science Digital Library Metadata Registry. http://metadataregistry.org.

> Links to registered RDA Element Sets and Value Vocabularies. http://metadataregistry.org/rdabrowse.htm.

### RDA Analysis

Antelman, Kristin. "Identifying the Serial Work as a Bibliographic Entity." *Library Resources and Technical Services* 48, no. 4 (Oct. 1, 2004): 238-255..

Coyle, Karen, and Diane Hillmann. "Resource Description and Access (RDA): Cataloging Rules for the 20th Century." *D-Lib Magazine* 13, no. 1/2 (Jan./Feb. 2007). www.dlib.org/dlib/january07/coyle/01coyle.html.

Library of Congress. "Testing Resource Description and Access (RDA)." www.loc.gov/bibliographic-future/rda.

Shadle, Steve. "FRBR and Serials." *Serials Librarian* 50, no. 1 & 2 (May 2006): 83-103.

## RDF

Dublin Core Metadata Initiative

> "DCMI Abstract Model." 2007. http://dublincore.org/documents/abstract-model.

> "Description Set Profiles: A Constraint Language for Dublin Core Application Profiles." 2008. http://dublincore.org/documents/dc-dsp.

> "Guidelines for Dublin Core Application Profiles." 2009. http://dublincore.org/documents/profile-guidelines/index.shtml.

> "The Singapore Framework for Dublin Core Application Profiles." 2008. http://dublincore.org/documents/singapore-framework.

Gradmann, Stefan. "rdfs:frbr—Towards an Implementation Model for Library Catalogs Using Semantic Web Technology." *Cataloging and Classification Quarterly* 39, no.3/4 (2005): 63-75.

"Resource Description Framework (RDF)." World Wide Web Consortium. 2004. www.w3.org/RDF.

## Linked Data

Berners-Lee, Tim. "Linked Data." 2006. www.w3.org/DesignIssues/LinkedData.html.

Linked Data. http://linkeddata.org.

World Wide Web Consortium. LinkingOpenData (Linked Data Task Force). http://esw.w3.org/topic/SweoIG/TaskForces/CommunityProjects/LinkingOpenData.

# Notes

# *Library Technology Reports* Respond to Your Library's Digital Dilemmas

Eight times per year, *Library Technology Reports* (LTR) provides library professionals with insightful elucidation, covering the technology and technological issues the library world grapples with on a daily basis in the information age.

| *Library Technology Reports* 2010, Vol. 46 | |
|---|---|
| **January** 46:1 | **"Understanding the Semantic Web: Bibliographic data and Metadata"** by Karen Coyle, Digital Library Consultant |
| **February/ March** 46:2 | **"RDA Vocabularies for a 21st-Century Data Environment"** by Karen Coyle, Digital Library Consultant |
| **April** 46:3 | **"Gadgets & Gizmos: Personal Electronics at your Library"** by Jason Griffey, Head of Library Information Technology, University of Tennessee at Chattanooga |
| **May/June** 46:4 | **"Object Re-Use and Exchange (OAI-ORE)"** by Mike Witt, Interdisciplinary Research Librarian & Assistant Professor of Library Science, Purdue University Libraries |
| **July** 46:5 | **"Web-Based Voice and Video: Investigating Library Applications and Challenges"** by Char Booth, E-Learning Librarian, University of California, Berkeley |
| **August/ September** 46:6 | **"Understanding Electronic Resources Usage: a Review of the State of the Art"** by Jill E. Grogg, E-Resources Librarian, University of Alabama Libraries, and Rachel Fleming-May, Assistant Professor, School of Information Sciences at the University of Tennessee |
| **October** 46:7 | **"Open URL"** by Cindi Trainor, Coordinator for Library Technology & Data Services at Eastern Kentucky University, and Jason Price, E-resource Package Analyst, Statewide California Electronic Library Consortium |
| **November/ December** 46:8 | **"Privacy and Freedom of Information in 21st Century Libraries"** by the ALA Office of Information Freedom, Chicago, IL |

www.alatechsource.org

ALA TechSource, a unit of the publishing department of the American Library Association

www.ingramcontent.com/pod-product-compliance
Lightning Source LLC
Chambersburg PA
CBHW080941300426
44115CB00017B/2901